Confessions of a Childless Mother

LEARNING TO TRUST GOD THROUGH INFERTILITY

First printed 2015

ISBN 978-1-84625-481-9

British Library Cataloguing in Publication Data available

Published by Day One Publications
Ryelands Road, Leominster, HR6 8NZ
☎ 01568 613 740 FAX 01568 611 473
email—sales@dayone.co.uk
web site—www.dayone.co.uk

Cover illustration by Rob Jones, Elk Design
Printed by TJ International

Endorsements

[illegible]

Sheila Stephen, lecturer in women's studies, Wales Evangelical School of Theology [illegible]

[illegible]

[illegible] Dr E. Bryn Davies, [illegible]

[illegible]

[illegible] Thomas, pastor of Alfred Place Baptist Church, Aberystwyth

Endorsements

This book is not an easy read, but it is an honest window into the painful world of infertility. In a society in which having a baby is often seen as a right, this is a reminder that life doesn't always turn out as we expect. The book is free from triumphalism and super-spirituality and at times borrows the language of lament. Those who struggle with this issue will find raw truth here and learn about the struggle to cope. It is a must for pastoral carers.

Sheila Stephen, Lecturer in women's issues at Wales Evangelical School of Theology (WEST)

My wife and I have struggled with infertility, like the author of this book and her husband. I welcome her honest, moving description of the longings, trauma, pain, struggles and encouragements experienced through infertility. If you are in this situation, you must read this excellent book; it will challenge and encourage you. Churches could distribute it to people, including leaders, to foster more, and much-needed, sensitivity and support for infertile couples. Read it—soon!

Rev. Dr D. Eryl Davies, Cardiff

During her three years at university in Aberystwyth, Sarah Fuller sat at my feet, as did her brother-in-law, and so my knowledge of the providences that this family have faced is first-hand. Yet in this narrative the testing experience of Sarah's childlessness was startling and moving to me. It has taught me to be a hundred times more tender and prayerful about this particular trial. The book is a history of the triumph of faith in a young woman whose hopes were set in a God whom she acknowledged had every right to fill her cup with whatever blend of sorrow and joy He saw fit to give her. This God sustained and rewarded her. From Him, and through Him, are all things, to whom be glory for ever.

Geoff Thomas, pastor of Alfred Place Baptist Church, Aberystwyth

Acknowledgements

There are many people to whom Nick and I have been indebted during the production of this book. We are thankful to God for you all.

We are deeply grateful to Matteo and Sarah, Matt and Sarah, Tertius and Julie, Nigel and Lois, Pete and Julie, Matt and Jayne, Peter and Joyce, Dave and Julie, Neil and Cat, Evan and Tracey, Charlie and Jenny, Ben and Julie, John and Katherine, Gary and Priya, Chris and Vanessa, Marcus and Mair, David and Fiona, Ray and Sharon, Bryan and Gill, Joe and Ali, Simon and Ruth, Jonathan and Abigail, Will and Sarah, Ian and Margaret, Keith and Chris, Dave and Ruth, Gareth and Annette, Jim and Anna, Graham and Sue, Daniel and Karen, Steve and Brenda, Bill and Sharon, Geoff and Iola, Tom and Natalie, Colin and Naomi, Peter and Sue, Olive, Janice, Tamsin, Jacqui, Carolyn, Helen, Martine, Sally Ann, Libby, Doris and Lynne for sharing your thoughts, feelings, insights and experiences, many of which are quoted and woven into the pages of this book. But thank you above all for supporting us as a couple and sharing your lives with us.

We are thankful to the congregations of Emmanuel Church, Leamington Spa, Bethel Baptist Church, Laleston, and Mirfield Evangelical Church for your steadfast love, prayers and care for us as we have walked this journey. Mirfield congregation, you in particular have loved, supported and prayed us through the greatest lows and highs of all. Thank you also to our new church family in Truro, who have prayed this book through to its completion.

I am thankful to Professor Jack Scarisbrick, Nuala Scarisbrick, and all my former colleagues at LIFE, especially those involved in the Life FertilityCare Programme. I am thankful for your integrity, support, expert knowledge and devotion to caring for us in our difficulties.

Many grateful thanks go to Lois Bryan, Judith Dennis, Julie Thorpe, Jacky Cooper, Dr Gillian Scothern, Vanessa Owen, Dr Sue Brown, Tirzah Jones, Dr Sharon James, Dr Eryl Davies, Gareth Williams and Ann Davies for reading through the manuscript and for your invaluable comments, advice, suggestions, additions and sheer determined encouragement for me to complete this work for publication. Lois, thank you for suggesting the title.

Particular thanks to Sheila Stephen for your unstinting support throughout the writing of this book, and for writing the counselling questions for the end of each chapter. Without your suggestion, this book would not have been written in the first place.

We are more thankful than we can ever express for the devoted love and support of our families throughout all the joys and trials of our lives—our parents, Bryan, Glyn, Mike and Chris; our brothers and their wives, John, Anne, Ian, Kath, Tim and Nici; and our nephews and nieces.

Finally, I give thanks to Nick, my loving, faithful and godly husband, who not only supported me in this enormous task of writing, but also gave much time, thought and effort to the production itself. I give special thanks to God for you.

Contents

Note from a childless father and husband

Sarah and I have been married for fourteen years, yet with no children. Infertility appears to be affecting an increasing proportion of people in the UK, to varying degrees. It is such a relevant issue today. The grief involved can be indescribably intense and unremitting. Yet the suffering may go unacknowledged by many others, and be misunderstood, sometimes leaving the sufferers without any meaningful help. Well-intended but misjudged comments and misplaced help unwittingly twist the knife yet further.

As Sarah and I have discovered, a professing Christian who struggles with infertility finds herself, or himself, struggling vehemently with none other than the sovereign God of providence. Driven to the unanswerable 'Why?' questions, they can find it easy to start sliding away from God. He seems to have let them down in a way most painful and devastating, and, for some, apparently in a manner designed to cause as much grief as possible. They may come to the conclusion that God does not love them, and is not good, kind or faithful. From our own experience we have learned that while struggling with infertility, and perhaps with God who allows and even plans the situation, it helps if others acknowledge our pain and give support to overcome it. Most of all, we need to collapse into the arms of our Comforter, and find Him to be our ever-present help in time of need.

In this Preface Sarah has asked me to give some reflections on our situation from my perspective as her husband. In our case the greater pain and suffering has been very much for Sarah than for myself. Childlessness causes me great grief at times, especially when I see happy families playing and laughing together. I always try not to dwell on my own pain, but to give thanks to God for their happiness. My difficulties have, largely, been of a different nature from my wife's. Sarah came to terms with our infertility but was soon after plunged into such desperate depths of grief, despair and hopelessness as tested and tried her faith to the limit. I have seen my beloved, godly wife struggling intensely with her heavenly Father, and in her confusion deeply questioning His love and goodness. As any loving husband would struggle to see his wife in severe physical pain, so my greatest suffering has been to see my wife in acute spiritual and emotional trauma. I have listened to Sarah cry out as Job did in the midst of his distress and perplexity, and have found it crushing. It is far easier to hear such words of struggle from someone with whom you are not intimately entwined. But Job's ultimate deliverance should have given me hope that God would ultimately deliver Sarah as well.

In addition, despite wanting to help my suffering wife, in the worst of our pain I sometimes felt utterly helpless in knowing how best to comfort Sarah. Words of Scripture that I tried to share under some circumstances perhaps came across as trite, maybe even critical. I have not always been able to pastor my own wife as I would have wished! One or two of the unhelpful comments to a person suffering from infertility that Sarah identifies I confess she has received from my own lips. Maybe sometimes it would have been best simply to emulate the initial response of Job's three friends, who began silent, and to hold Sarah patiently until the pain eased. Perhaps there is a lesson there for the one who suffers less pain than their spouse in their infertility, however well meaning they may be.

As her husband, I have tried to help Sarah in her grief. My thoughts have been for her more than for my own pain in childlessness. I imagined that I needed to be the rock on which Sarah could lean and rely. As she has gradually risen from her depths, so I have felt better able to express my own sorrow. On reflection, perhaps that expression would have provided more help to Sarah had I let more of it surface earlier, alongside hers. It is God who is our Rock, and He wants us to rely on Him in our distress. Maybe it would be helpful if we husbands let our wives know our real feelings and pain a little more.

So I have seen and experienced how much pain and suffering infertility can cause, and especially to one who aches to be a mother. But God has brought us both through. As with Job, He did not let Sarah go. The graciousness, acceptance and faith with which she now writes are a powerful testimony purely to the strength and effectiveness of God's ongoing healing. Furthermore, as Sarah has been enabled to write this book I have seen clearly how powerful God's grace is. He has raised her from the brink of near collapse to a deeper, enriched faith in Him and His Word, and love for Him. I myself have learned more fully to appreciate that Job's questioning of God was a normal (if still, in parts, sinful) human response to overwhelming grief. God Himself has held Sarah and me together, and as we slowly come out the other end, we find that He has strengthened our marriage and deepened our bonds of love.

We both pray that God may use this book to give comfort and encouragement to those who are unhappily childless. This is not just for women. Men struggling with infertility will also, we trust, find some help. Husbands who want to understand and support their grieving wives will also find invaluable suggestions. Those who desire to walk alongside a suffering couple in this trial might benefit from being educated and informed about the deep sufferings of infertility, so they can offer genuine sympathy and effective help.

Nick Fuller

Introduction

It was several years ago now. At the beginning of a ladies' Bible study group we had each been asked to define 'who' or 'what' we were. What, in a nutshell, defined me?

As the question moved around the circle, I kept hearing from the many women there: 'I am a mother.' The thought came unbidden to my mind: 'I am a *childless* mother.' Swiftly I brushed the jolting pain aside. 'I am a child of God' came my response, quite genuine, to the waiting group. But it had reopened a train of thought to me. You see, I had always thought of myself as a 'mother'. I feel 'motherly', with strong maternal instincts. But Nick and I, both now approaching forty, have no children.

We fall into the category of the almost one in six couples in the UK who experience problems conceiving. Of these, about 30 per cent apparently fall into the category of 'unexplained infertility'. This deeply frustrating situation is one in which doctors have been unable to diagnose any definite problem, yet the couple continually fail to conceive. Nick and I were in this very painful position for nine years, and are now in it again, as I shall explain later. We also know many other couples, mostly Christian, who for various reasons are childless when they do not wish to be so. As much as the couples differ, so do their diagnoses, feelings and experiences.

This written account of our childlessness began life in late 2009, originally planned in response to a requested magazine article. However, infertility is such a complex subject, and over the months, as my pain spilled out, so the 'article' grew. It grew yet further when I began to consider everything that God has done to help us, and it became too large for a magazine. This book is the result. It is written mostly from my feminine perspective, but this is very much Nick's story too. He has written not only the Preface, but also the prayers at the end of the chapters. He is therefore present throughout.

He has read through the manuscript in minute detail, discussing the content and helping me in my search to understand and apply biblical truth to our painful circumstances.

Of course, there are other good resources already available and some of them are mentioned in the appendices. I have read all the books listed and found them helpful over the years. I am not trying to rival these books, although I am aware that some of the themes they contain may have been echoed subconsciously in my own work. But in recording our personal story, Nick and I are most concerned that those who are struggling may at least realize that they are not alone: others also feel, and have felt, the same or similar hurts. But this is a book of hope too. We are also keen to share how God has helped us over the years. We want to encourage infertile couples that they can reach out for a hand to grasp theirs when they are finding life tough or even unbearable, and that there is eventually light at the end of the tunnel. Despite how it may seem at times, when we experience God's faithful love and the care of others, infertility does not have to be the end of life as we know it.

The questions, Bible verses and prayers at the end of each chapter are designed to help couples focus on ways they can work through their personal painful situation of infertility, perhaps with each other, a friend or a counsellor. We also want to re-emphasize our hope that this book will give some insight into the situation for those who care about an infertile couple. They may find Chapters 6 and 7 particularly relevant.

Part 1 Our story

Part 1

I had always wanted to be a wife and mother. In fact, throughout my childhood, teenage years and early twenties I had never really been able to envisage my future life in any other way. I was not hugely career-minded (although I wanted work which would involve children, perhaps as a doctor or teacher, and then more unusually wished to be a vicar's wife!). My older brother and I were brought up in a loving Christian home where our parents were good role models for us, and we both professed faith in Jesus when we were children. There was also a great sadness in our younger days. I was aged six when our dearly loved baby brother died from cot death just six weeks after his birth. I have often wondered since if this tragic curtailing of my 'big sisterly' affections developed in me a stronger yearning to nurture others. Alongside this, my own love for 'little ones' seems to have developed at a very early stage. Even as a very young child, I always wanted to hold new babies and was fascinated by their development. As I got older, I loved looking after our friends' and neighbours' small children. I wanted to have lots of children myself. When starting secondary school, I would borrow books about baby and child development from the school library—though that wasn't considered very cool by some of my classmates, as you may imagine! Several friends have commented since on how much my unusual love of little children was apparent from an early age.

After leaving university I qualified as a primary teacher, and enjoyed the opportunities it gave to be involved in the lives and training of young children. Nick and I married in our mid-twenties and from the start we were in agreement about wanting children and about how many we hoped to have. So just over a couple of years after our wedding, at the beginning of the year 2000, we were excited, though also a little overawed, at the prospect of trying for a family of our own. We had no real reason to suspect there might be any problem. We felt ready to be parents. We had committed the situation to God in prayer from the beginning and we were both healthy. I had even wondered with some poignancy if I'd had a very early miscarriage when we had been living abroad the year before (I had not done a test).

After a year of our trying but not conceiving, and of becoming somewhat perplexed and anxious, our GP sent us for tests. These were conducted over a number of months; some were repetitive, painful and invasive. Our life became anxiously and confusingly full of hospitals, and it was increasingly hard to think about much else. We were finally advised after several months of very nervous waiting that my position was such that I would almost certainly never conceive a child naturally. It was such an unexpected blow that I became faint. We both staggered from that clinic in a daze. My whole world almost fell apart that night. Over the next weeks I experienced the common symptoms of bereavement: waking in the night with a knot of pain gnawing in the pit of my stomach and dread filling my heart. Feelings of denial, loss and disbelief constantly swept over me throughout my waking hours. I seemed at first to cry continually, sometimes uncontrollably, and until there were no tears left; I questioned, desperately prayed for a miracle, and truly wondered how God, our heavenly Father, could allow us to go through such intense pain. Did He not love us? Were children not a blessing we were supposed to desire? Did the Bible not say so? Was God saying there was something terribly wrong with us as a couple or with our Christian lives? In painful contrast, many other friends, relatives and church members around us seemed to be constantly falling pregnant with ease.

However, as time passed we became increasingly unhappy with the diagnosis, as some details just did not add up, and we opted for a second laparoscopy at a private clinic. This was under a top specialist in the field in which we had been told was the problem. After a very careful search, this kind and helpful consultant gave us a completely opposite diagnosis: that actually there was nothing really wrong and that we should expect to have a baby within the year! Of course we were delighted, with our hopes happily renewed. The joyful news eventually faded into distant memory, though, as we then endured another couple of years during which our hopes were painfully dashed with never-ending monthly disappointments.

Eventually we opted for the LIFE FertilityCare Programme (LFP). This is a private treatment option that has connections with the charity LIFE, and is a family-friendly, ethical approach. It is a positive alternative to standard reproductive technologies. We were treated with great care and respect as deeply valued people. In fact, after my initial contact with the FertilityCare practitioner, I wept—but this time with relief, because I felt that at last somebody had taken my concerns seriously and offered hope. They diagnosed a completely different problem, which was addressed. However, after carefully following the programme for a couple of years, we sadly realized it was not going to work for us. Nobody really knows why the programme did not succeed in our case, as it has for many others. From a human point of view, and as far as we could see, it should have done. However, I do believe that we received a measure of emotional healing simply from being cared for so devotedly by the LFP over those few years.

So, finally, after six very turbulent years since we had begun trying for a baby, the final diagnosis appeared to be 'unexplained infertility'. Two years later, in 2008, we finally turned down the possibility of any invasive and uncertain treatment on the NHS. We had by then decided that a continued focus on trying to get pregnant was unhelpful. It was with much sadness, yet also certainty that God has us in His hands and always does the best for us, that we turned our thoughts away from our treasured dream of a family. I had given up the teaching a number of years before, hoping that the reduction of stress might make a difference (obviously it had not). I had, however, been working for LIFE as an Education Officer in local schools. We had by this time also been through WEST Bible College, two moves, and were firmly settled in our present church where God had called Nick to be the pastor.

I had always believed, even as a young teenager, that infertility was a problem I would never be able to cope with. How could I, when I had such strong maternal feelings, and all I had really envisaged long-term was being a mother? And yet eventually, somehow, God did do the impossible. By about August 2008, eight and a half years after our infertility story began, I realized there was a difference. I had been given peace in my soul over this situation that God had led us into. God gave me total satisfaction in knowing that He was in control, and that He never makes mistakes. In talking it all through with Nick, I realized we both felt the same. We would probably never hold the baby in our arms that we so longed for, but our thoughts were turned to heaven, and we were heading for that. We trusted that God had some different work for us now, rather than having a family. It was not that I had stopped *wanting* to be a mother, and I am not saying that little reminders would not now and again stab at me. But I was no longer aching or even hoping each month for a baby, as we had truly given up the idea that it would ever happen. I was able to be happy for other pregnant women, and enabled to talk freely again to mothers about their pregnancies, babies and children. Nick was well settled in the busy ministry of our new church and I had begun working again part-time, for LIFE. This was work I loved and in which I felt confident: teaching to various public groups the importance of valuing life before birth, and other ethical issues. Our lives finally seemed full of hope and purpose, and I was deeply grateful to the Lord for this joyful contentment after those years of uncertainty, turmoil and misery.

But then in January 2009, I fell pregnant. It seemed like a miracle. We laughed and cried as we held the test, that unbelievable blue cross which was so clear. I had been feeling very different for a couple of weeks, but we had scarcely dared to believe it could be this. Who would ever have thought it? Had our 'turn' really come at last? It was such a precious time together as we made tentative early plans and shared our joy with immediate family and just a few close friends. Knowing that some long-term infertile women who eventually conceive may also be at higher risk of miscarriage we began to pray earnestly for the life within: that it would grow healthily and be born safely. We also prayed, as so many Christian couples do, that God would use this child for His glory.

However, all was not straightforward. Even in the very early stages I had begun to experience slight, intermittent bleeding. After about five weeks this subsided, and as everything began to look positive (blood test results were very good), we started to relax just a little, and to risk anticipating the future. All along I was simply amazed at how such a tiny being could have such a profound impact upon my body and mind. But by seven weeks the bleeding had begun again, and I was also anxiously experiencing a strange pain on one side of my abdomen. We urged the prayers of those who knew, and were booked in for an early, eight weeks ultrasound, as some doctors feared an ectopic pregnancy. To our enormous distress the scan was very unclear. Thankfully, the pregnancy sac was in the uterus, but our situation still did not look good. So we had to wait two agonizing weeks for another scan, with untold dread and desperate prayers. The following ten weeks scan confirmed what we had increasingly suspected and yet could barely face. Our precious little one had stopped developing at an undisclosed early stage. The situation was classified as a 'missed miscarriage' because I had not yet physically lost the baby and, ironically, had long stopped bleeding by then. I was given surgery the next day.

The pregnancy and subsequent trauma have left me with some ongoing physical problems. But they are small compared with the enormous emotional, mental and spiritual devastation. The rawness of the resulting pain and grief are hard to describe adequately. As we left the hospital after the final scan on that bleak early March afternoon, complete with instructions about the following day's operation, we needed to cross a busy main road. As a bus rolled by directly in front of us I fleetingly wondered if it could feel any worse were I actually under its wheels. I had tumbled into total spiritual darkness. I was as if suspended over a chasm, and completely surrounded by its blackness. For those first few hours I could not pray or concentrate on anything at all. I could not listen to anything or anyone. At home and lying on our sofa, I could hear myself wailing, but even that seemed far off and distant. After the operation I felt especially empty, as if a part of me had been lost with our child. It felt like our brief happiness had been heartlessly mocked. The whole situation just felt so very cruel—especially given that, after so many years of suffering infertility, we had finally found peace. I was angry, I felt it was unfair, but mostly my heart was just shattered, as if it had been torn out and crushed underfoot. I saw no purpose to my life any more. I had an overwhelming longing for our baby, already so loved by us, and my arms and heart ached with emptiness. I wondered how I would ever get over this, and feared that it could be the final event that would send me into complete emotional instability.

The 'why' questions were overflowing. Why did God give life, only to take it away again so soon after it had begun? Why did He allow this unexpected hope to blossom when at last we had found a blessed measure of contentment and peace in our childless situation? Why had that then been snatched away? Why did God not answer our fervent prayers for our baby's life? A couple of times during the pregnancy we had joked to each other that this was surely all too good to be true. Now, ironically, that really seemed to be so. I was also filled with feelings of vague guilt. Was it because of something we had done, or not done? There was no apparent answer.

Furthermore, in strange and painful contrast to our own situation, there were *many* pregnancies of which we suddenly became aware, with the babies due at almost exactly the same time ours would have been. All of these were of dear family members, friends, colleagues and people in our church network. I gave up counting how many new babies were expected, but it seemed as if Nick and I alone had been singled out for misery. Why were others able to have a baby (even many babies) and yet us not even one? The expectant couples, of course, were themselves extremely distressed by the situation. Many expressed their grief and sorrow for us with great love and sensitivity, and we felt for them in their awkwardness: it was just so difficult for us all. But it also seemed, however, that somewhere, someone was making things almost as hard as they could be for Nick and me at that time. Without focusing on the details there just seemed to be so many little twists in the whole situation which turned the knife even more, compounding our heartache. In the few years since, many more new babies have been expected and born to others we know and love. Some have been to couples that in the past also suffered miscarriages and infertility but who are happily now parents. We are pleased for all of them, but I have found it a confusing and lonely time.

As those early weeks after the miscarriage moved by I also found that to continue with the job at LIFE was just too traumatic for me. It was now barely possible to present photographs of unborn and newborn babies, and discuss their development in public, without either breaking down or hardening myself and denying my feelings, which I thought to be unhealthy. Yet, in finishing that employment I experienced another loss: that of some purpose for my life in a work where I had wonderful understanding colleagues and for a cause that I care passionately about. I therefore also lost an important form of practical distraction. It was a desperately dark time.

Mercifully, my initial experience of complete blackness was confined only to those first few days. Yet the following months were still impossibly difficult. While coping externally perhaps, internally I was, as another friend described herself after a very similar trauma, 'barely functional', and was sometimes dropping into complete desperation. I finally reached my first level 'plateau' about eighteen months after the operation.

It is difficult to recall these painful details. I still think of that little one, all these years later, and wonder how our lives would be had the outcome been different. Even now, we still definitely have our moments, and I have times of deep questioning and troughs of depression. Thinking in any detail about these events can still cause me to cry.

Honestly, I still wonder why God allowed it all to be so acutely and peculiarly painful. I am, however, beginning to be enabled to say again to God, 'Your will be done.' I have begun again to trust that God is defined by love and graciousness, that His plans are always for our good, and that He never does anything wrong or unjust. Even in the darkest of days following the operation, God was there, giving us little indications of His care for us, gently reminding us that we were not forgotten, that He was in control. Despite everything, we have come a long way since those events of early 2009. God has graciously blessed me with new and interesting work, which has given me some helpful diversion, and sympathetic new colleagues. We both know that we have much to live for, together as a couple and in our service of God. Quite simply, God has brought us through this far.

However, one of the hardest aspects of it all is that, after being blessed with that amazing peace before the miscarriage, I have become just as desperate, if not more so, to have a baby as I was all those years ago. My contentment has not yet been fully regained. Many dear friends encourage us that as we have conceived once, why not again? Of course we had our hopes renewed a little. But it took so *long* to conceive: nine years! In another nine years we shall surely be too old. In fact, our situation is even harder now because we are much older. We do not actually know why the miscarriage happened, as due to understandable financial constraints doctors will not usually refer a woman for investigations until she has experienced three such confirmed pregnancy losses in a row. We simply do not know whether we shall ever be able to conceive again; we have not since. Hopes renewed but not fulfilled have been indescribably painful. We are living again with the monthly cycle of them being raised but then horribly dashed. One consultant informed us recently that very little research has been done on the actual causes of infertility since the 1980s. However, after such a long period without conceiving, it seems to the medical profession that there must be something wrong with either Nick or myself, or with both of us. They have suggested likely possibilities. But as more detailed testing is currently unavailable, we will probably never know in this life the true physical cause of our problem, or what could be done on a human level to solve it.

So now we are dealing with the particular grief of having lost our unborn child (dates were very difficult, especially the due date), but also, once again, with all the emotions associated with infertility. These previously experienced difficulties, which we thought had been laid to rest, have returned in full force. We live with the trust that in time, God will completely restore the peace that was shattered. We also entrust to Him the tiny life that was lost to us, thanking Him for the brief time of joy it brought us both. We are attempting to relearn lessons previously learnt.

So it is with our experience in mind that I now attempt to describe in further detail how long-term infertility has affected us as a couple, and especially me as a childless woman. Infertility will be the focus of this book, rather than miscarriage, which is such a major issue that it needs to be dealt with separately. Of course, there are several different ways in which people experience unwanted childlessness. Now that we have certainly conceived, we are technically classed as suffering with 'secondary infertility'. But because we have no children living, and do not seem to be able to conceive again, all our original infertility 'issues' remain. We also have a number of single friends who long (or have longed) to be both married and parents; some of the women especially struggle, knowing potential childbearing years are slipping away. Some friends have just one child and do not seem able to conceive another (again known as 'secondary infertility'). Others have conceived quickly but endured multiple miscarriages, and so have no living children. All of these will perhaps be able to relate to some of the issues raised in this book. As with any traumatic situation, each couple's experiences and feelings about it will differ. We also know couples who have never had children but for whom it has not been a great problem. Their thoughts and encouragements have also been helpful to us.

The next section of the book, 'Part 2. Hurts of the Childless', comes with a caveat. It is a long description of the very painful circumstances which we and many other childless couples have endured. It may be upsetting for some readers. If you find it too distressing, do turn on to 'Part 3. Help for the Childless', which attempts to apply some meaningful help to couples facing these enormous trials, and also gives ideas for how friends and pastoral carers can help them.

Part 2 Hurts of the childless

Chapter 1

Spiritual struggles

For Christian couples suffering infertility, the spiritual aspect of the trial can perhaps be hardest of all. Our loving God, whom we trust, and for whom we seek to live faithful lives, has denied us one of His greatest earthly blessings. Why? Lois Flowers, author of a very helpful book on infertility (the first I ever read on the subject, over nine years ago), wrote,

> For some reason, perhaps because God created us with an innate desire to create and nurture, the inability to have a baby often seems to pose greater challenges to our faith and emotions than other difficult trials we might encounter in our lives. We've been taught all our lives that children are a blessing from the Lord; so why wouldn't He want us to enjoy His blessings like everyone else around us?[I]

As we believe that God is Sovereign Creator of the universe and the author of all life, we know that He could, in the blink of an eye, give us the child we so long for. He gives children to most Christians (indeed, most people), whether they had initially wanted them or not. We know that He can and does perform 'miracles' in many people's childless situations. Some infertile people feel that God must not really love them as much as He does other Christians, or that He has actually abandoned them. Has He forgotten to be gracious and merciful? Has He simply forgotten them altogether? Or are these couples unsuitable, substandard Christians in some way? The issue can lead some struggling couples to begin doubting whether God is actually in control at all, or whether He is as loving as they had thought.

A blessing withheld

Many childless Christian couples know in their heart of hearts that the real reason they do not have children (regardless of any medical condition) is because *God* has not enabled them to conceive. It seems that He has not planned for them to raise a family of their own. The Old Testament believers were well aware of God's sovereignty in this area of life. Many times in the Bible we read words like '[God] opened her womb' or 'had closed her womb' (such as in Gen. 29–30), or 'the LORD enabled her to conceive' (Ruth 4:13). When Rachel strongly expressed her infertility misery to Jacob, he exclaimed back to her in frustration, 'Am I in the place of God, who has kept you from having children?' (Gen. 30:2). Likewise, the patriarch Abraham cried out to God in Genesis 15:3 (before he was given the promise of Isaac), 'You have given me no children; so a servant in my household will be my heir.'

Many sincerely wonder why God keeps from some faithful Christian couples this precious blessing of children which is pointedly described as such in the Bible. This is especially so in the Old Testament. For example, consider Psalm 127:3–5:

> Sons are a heritage from the LORD,
> children a reward from him.
> Like arrows in the hands of a warrior
> are sons born in one's youth.
> Blessed is the man
> whose quiver is full of them.

Verses such as these can pierce the hearts of those unsuccessfully trying to conceive. The Bible seems to set such importance on being physically 'fruitful'. Moreover, why does God allow such painful comparisons with others, or sometimes allow hopes to be raised, for them only to be dashed? Why does He give some couples a strong desire to bear and raise children, but never provide the fulfilment of this? Would it not at least have been better for those who were to be infertile to have been created without such strong maternal/paternal feelings? Surely God could have done this?

Struggles with unanswered prayer

Many Christian childless couples wonder why God does not answer their persistent and fervent prayers for a baby, especially when many other Christians have also been praying faithfully for them. These prayers may have been the broken-hearted pleadings of many years. When others conceive easily around them, such infertile couples can feel entirely overlooked by God. This can even be difficult when another couple struggling with long-term infertility finally conceive and give birth. Joyful and perhaps encouraging though this event may be, the still-childless couple can really begin to think there is something wrong with them or their prayers. They wonder, 'Why did God finally answer this other couple's prayers, but never ours?' Surely it is such a simple, even 'normal' request? So many feel utterly confused. I vividly remember, during an especially dark time, saying to a friend, 'I wouldn't wish this pain on *anyone* ... I have prayed and prayed for it to be taken away, so why does my loving heavenly Father still put this upon me? I am meant to be His much-loved child!'

Some then find they are tempted to see conception as just a random event in the world, as those who yearn and perhaps earnestly pray for years to have a baby never do conceive, while some others who certainly did not wish to be pregnant become so. It seems so desperately unfair and mismatched. And why do some really lovely Christian couples have many children, perhaps in answer to prayer, while others, equally lovely, equally suitable, never have any, despite all the prayers? To our human eyes it really makes no sense at all. If God is in control of all this, why does He allow, or even designate, such painful inequality in this matter, even among His own people?

Are infertile couples spiritual failures?

Some infertile couples fear that God is judging them or has found their marriage to be lacking in some way. Perhaps they wonder if God is punishing them for some sin of the past, or possibly of the present, or even for a subconscious sin. Worse still, some have others (usually those with children themselves) actually say such things to them. Sometimes the people around them will suggest that an infertile couple's faith is too weak in some way, or that they are not praying hard enough. What an unfair pressure that can be, at an already painful and confusing time. Most couples struggling with all the spiritual, physical and emotional issues of infertility have prayed constantly for God to change their situation; to bless them in this, should that be His will. Thus some become utterly worn out and discouraged in prayer altogether, as God simply does not answer all such prayers positively.

Most infertile couples can never see such a reason why God should have withheld children from them, and they are confused. As one childless friend reflected, 'Surely it is a noble thing to want?'—to love and give yourself wholeheartedly and selflessly in the bringing up of a family? Aren't there few enough people in the world these days prepared to do this? Surely it is not a selfish thing to desire? It is hardly comparable with lusting after wealth, or fame, or power, is it?

Struggles in church

For a struggling infertile couple, even attending church can be very hard as there are often many apparently happy families who seem to be greatly blessed by God, and some who will tell us so in their great joy. Sometimes there are several large and ever-increasing generations of a particular family in one church alone. Often there can be several new babies expected and born every year. Much obvious attention can be given to the new babies and their proud parents in a general church setting and sometimes in the church services themselves. Furthermore, the Christian world is very small. So even if there are not many babies expected in a couple's own church, it is very likely that they will often be hearing on the grapevine of other Christian couples who are expecting or who have had children. The contrast in situations can seem unbridgeable. One (fertile) friend commented to me that she thinks infertility must be especially hard for Christian couples. She remarked how, if they did not go to church, a couple could choose to manage their pain quite effectively by avoiding young families altogether. They could seek out hotels, pursuits and other social situations where children were not present with their parents, and where they did not have to witness close at hand the differences in their situations. If a church seems to be especially centred around family and children's work, the childless can feel totally excluded and useless in the very place they should feel most at home. Even singing emotional hymns about God's goodness and love can set a person off in tears when perhaps they are struggling at that time to believe that God cares about them and their situation at all.

So some infertile couples can begin to wonder if God hears their prayers, or perhaps whether He has forgotten to answer, whether He is being unkind, whether He is able to help them, or even whether He is there at all. Such unresolved spiritual issues concerning God's goodness and love can eventually lead to deeply entrenched bitterness and resentment. Many of us struggling with infertility will admit how all the varied trials of this long-term issue can at the very least diminish our joy in the Lord and even in our salvation. It is an overwhelming problem. I have known several infertile Christians who over time have lost their impetus in the Lord's work, some who have begun to backslide, and a few who have tragically fallen away from their Christian faith altogether.

Some of the ways God has helped us through our spiritual struggles can be found in Chapters 7 and 12.

Pause for thought

Try to answer these questions as honestly as possible.

- What are your thoughts, feelings and beliefs about your current situation?
- In what ways has your current situation led to spiritual doubts?
- Have you shared these doubts with anyone? If not, why not?
- Pray about the first step you can take to cope with your doubts.

Bible passages for reflection

As you do not know the path of the wind,
  or how the body is formed in a mother's womb,
so you cannot understand the work of God,
  the Maker of all things. (Eccles. 11:5)

I am still confident of this:
  I will see the goodness of the LORD
  in the land of the living.
Wait for the LORD;
  be strong and take heart
  and wait for the LORD. (Ps. 27:13–14)

Prayer

Sovereign Lord God, you are the God of providence. You rule the universe. You rule my life. You decide everything that happens to me. I can't fathom your ways; they are beyond my understanding. Sometimes it seems that you overlook me. Sometimes it seems that you are not listening to my requests. Sometimes I'm tempted to doubt that you love me. I can't understand why you allow the suffering I go through. Please, loving Father, help me to trust you. Help me to trust that you are in control. Help me to understand that you know best, and that your plans are perfect. Help me truly to believe that you love me. O God, I ask you, keep me from sliding away from you. In your mercy, Amen.

Chapter 2

Emotional trauma

There are not words adequate to describe how it feels to be unhappily infertile or to explain the desolation that can be experienced. One writer began a booklet on the subject with the words, 'The destructive power of childlessness, an anguish which, concealed from the world in general, will manifest itself in all manner of physical and mental disorder …'[1] When I discussed this book with one childless friend (who has now adopted a family of children) she emphasized having never suffered so much in her life so far as with this trial. She well remembers the feelings of total inadequacy, failure and lack of control in the situation; of wants and needs which are never fulfilled; the endless sobbing until she could hardly breathe any more. She recalls how, in the worst of it, she would wake every morning and wonder, 'Will I ever think about anything else? Will I ever have a "normal" thought again?'

Another young woman's story, recorded by author Beth Spring in her booklet *Childless*, will resonate painfully in the hearts of most other infertile women. The unnamed writer remembered,

> I cried inside almost constantly, and the slightest nudge to my emotions would bring the tears out … One day, while driving, I noticed a woman in the car ahead of me talking to a baby in a car seat. Stopped at a red light, she was pointing out sights by the road as the baby's tiny fists bounced excitedly up and down. I cried so hard I could hardly continue driving.[2]

These are just two brief examples from countless others I could include.

The Bible does not minimize the anguish of this trial. In helping us understand the experience of infertility, the book *Just the Two of Us?*

refers to a biblical description of the raw and strength-sapping emotions involved. It is found in Proverbs 30:15b–16 and I too quote it in full:

> There are three things that are never satisfied,
> four that never say, 'Enough!':
> the grave, the barren womb,
> land, which is never satisfied with water,
> and fire, which never says, 'Enough!'

The book goes on to explain,

> Think about those TV images of raging forest fires that we see every summer, consuming everything in their paths, or the famine-struck desert on the news, ready to soak up any amount of water you could pour on it. They are images for us to ponder on so that we might have an insight into the psychology of infertility. Facing childlessness can be a consuming, hungry and ravaging experience, which can threaten to overpower the strongest faith.[3]

Bereavement

I believe that infertility is actually a form of chronic bereavement for many couples. Those whose hopes for a family have been shattered often undergo responses similar to those experienced after losing a loved one. They can include various forms of shock, denial, helplessness, uncontrollable crying, anger, depression, hopelessness, purposelessness, emptiness, a constant searching, despair, loss of various appetites, struggling with sleep, and just wondering how to get through the next day (not to mention the rest of life).

They realize that something utterly precious and irreplaceable has been taken from them (although not in the 'usual' way), and often wonder if life can ever hold any joy again, or if it is indeed worth living at all. These symptoms can be more keenly felt in the wake of a shock infertility diagnosis, but years of constant disappointment with no real answers can also result in them. Do you remember Hannah's agony, as recorded for us in 1 Samuel 1? When praying in the temple and then speaking with Eli, she is described as being in much 'bitterness of soul', in 'misery', 'deeply troubled', in 'great anguish and grief' and 'downcast'. Hannah, of course, was struggling with the added torments of her husband's (fertile) other wife. But many infertile women would profoundly identify with Hannah's emotions. Some on the outside of an infertility situation may wonder about the grieving, thinking that those who have never conceived have not actually lost anything definable. But the couple have truly lost much, albeit in less tangible ways, and grieve deeply in response to that loss. As one Hospital Counselling Service pamphlet helpfully summarizes it, 'There is the loss of the potential child, the loss of the parenting experience, the loss of control in some areas of their life, and perhaps, the loss of a particular self-image, in view of the great value placed on parenthood in our society.'[4]

One friend, after trying unsuccessfully to conceive for a couple of years, confided, 'This is worse than when my father died.' That was significant, because he was a much-loved father who had died tragically and suddenly when my friend was only seventeen. Her honest revelation was helpful because it enabled me to understand a little of why I was feeling so awful. For some infertile couples, the bereavement of infertility may well be the most traumatic grief they will ever experience. Obviously, this will not be so for all. We hope that anyone suffering any form of bereavement or loss will receive support from others who understand the pain, but one common difficulty with infertility is that many in this position feel totally misunderstood. It is not, after all, a 'normal' form of bereavement. It can seem to an infertile couple that all their joy in life and hopes for the future have been robbed, leaving them cowering in a pile of ashes. But it often appears to them (sometimes from bitter experience) that there are very few people who really appreciate the immensity of the problem, or recognize the depths of grief it can bring. Who will truly understand their devastation and disappointment, or acknowledge the depth of their heart's yearnings, their fears, their empty yet still aching arms, and their utter confusion?

One difference with infertility grieving compared with most other forms is that there is no real focus for the grief, such as a funeral and the attendant public recognition of the loss. In the case of those who have never conceived at all, they have no memories to comfort them and no hope of a future reunion. There are no photographs; there is not even a name to remember with tenderness. But the couple are bereft of all the children they longed for and prayed to have. Sometimes in our house it can seem as if there is something missing. I occasionally look around our dining table when Nick and I are there alone and think of the little faces I had hoped would be sitting with us. Or I look at happy families when I am out and about, and wonder how ours would have been. It is desperate to realize that these long-cherished dreams are fading away and may never be realized. It is unbelievably painful to accept that all the love stored up, which we are aching to share, may never find release in caring for our own baby. Just occasionally, and at differing times, both Nick and I have dreamed at night that we actually have a baby, whom we love. Life seems especially empty when we awake after such vivid dreams. There can be the feeling of trying to find that child, of trying to hold on to what has disappeared in the morning light.

One friend describes these disturbing and empty feelings as her 'unsettled ghosts' and wonders, 'What are we to do with the unfulfilled love, the unrequited, unplaced love, which we have to give, but cannot express, due to our circumstances?' Many women in particular have a deeply inbuilt desire to nurture others, and this is usually fulfilled in raising their own families. How can a woman satisfy this part of her nature if no family comes along?

Another extremely difficult aspect of the 'bereavement' for many couples still hoping for a baby is that infertility is not one decisive event. The experience of loss, pain and hopelessness returns in unremitting full force every month. Every month, as the couple's emotions restabilize after a previous disappointment, hope begins to rise with the woman's oestrogen levels. Then they reach what is known as the 'fertile time', and hope against hope that *this* time might be THE month. As the days continue they might even begin to think, perhaps by some deceptively positive symptoms or a longer wait than usual, that they finally have a reason to anticipate a joyful outcome. But then they are disappointed yet again. And every time this happens they can be knocked back into a deepening chasm of failure and desperation. One man revealed that some months he felt as if their feelings were being 'played with'. Once they had a wait of an extra two weeks, which was most unusual for them. Their hopes were high—but no, then it all came crashing down around them, and it was almost unbearable. As another friend describes it, 'From the heights of hope to the depths of despair, every single month.' Yet another friend confessed, 'My husband always knew it was bad news, as he would find me sobbing on the toilet.'

Imagine how this cycle of heartbreak, when suffered long-term, will affect the minds, emotions and spirits of the couples who bear it. Naturally the realization of failure occurs at the time when many women are also struggling with PMT and are feeling more vulnerable than usual. Such a situation is exhausting in every respect. The proverb 'Hope deferred makes the heart sick' (Prov. 13:12) is painfully real to those in this situation. It can indeed feel as if their emotions are being cruelly tormented. Occasionally I have thought—and I write this very carefully—that the daily wait each month can sometimes feel like a form of mental torture. Depression, with all its attendant symptoms, can really set in when this grief and uncertainty continue indefinitely.

As with other bereavements, the wounds will often reopen and bleed; pain and tears can return very suddenly, when least expected, sometimes after weeks, months or even years of calm acceptance. All will eventually reach the end of their childbearing years. They may or may not have found peace by this time, but here too, as Katherine Hall points out, 'There is no programme, no formal method of helping the couple through this very final anguish.'[5]

Painful comparisons with others

Just when a couple realize again that they are not expecting, they may hear the joyful news that someone else is; perhaps someone close to them in their work, church, neighbourly or family situation and whom they might see throughout the months of pregnancy. There are those who have just been given a devastating, possibly permanent, diagnosis of infertility who then discover that their dearest friend, colleague or sibling (someone to whom they would naturally turn for help and support) is happily expecting a baby. During their potential childbearing years an infertile couple may constantly be surrounded by news of such pregnancies and births. They may be buying presents and cards, seeing photos, reading news of and watching many dear little children grow up who are not their own. One friend described how she experiences a sharp physical pain on hearing about a new pregnancy, never her own. Indeed, it can feel like a punch in the stomach.

Many a childless woman will feel the pressure to attend social events such as baby showers, which are becoming so popular today, for happily pregnant women. She fears being perceived as jealous and a killjoy if she does not attend. However, if she does join in, she wonders where to look, not wanting any eye contact with those there. She fears she might cry.

She fears suffocating under her stifled emotions. Everyone is, naturally, discussing the adorable little presents and their uses. The childless woman will think they are cute too, but she may also want to run away and bawl. I have felt really embarrassed and have almost panicked at such occasions in the past. (I have one childless friend who fears that pre-birth baby showers are rather 'dangerous' anyway, as the child is not yet born and some individuals can conceive and have a problem-free pregnancy right up until the last stages, when there are complications.)

Much as the infertile couple may love those concerned and want to be glad for a newly pregnant couple, the contrast in situations can be almost too painful to bear. They know how they will struggle to see the happiness and expectancy on the couple's faces, and to see the excitement bloom with the new mother's blossoming figure. They know that it will hurt to see the parental pride and joy when the little one is born, and the parents' pride in each other too, as love and tender care is poured out on the child. They are aware of missing out on the growing confidence, maturity, respect from society and new experiences that come with being parents; the funny and tender memories that will be treasured, laughter and activity in the home as the child grows up, and even the close and loving relationships that many adults enjoy with their grown children. Women especially may be aware how it is often declared that there is no human love greater than that of a mother for her child. Some will urge mothers that no one else can ever love her children as much as she does. A hurting childless woman will wonder why she will perhaps never know that love. Many older parents will insist that the years when their children were young were the happiest of their entire lives. It is all that a childless couple yearn for and yet have so far been denied. The future of an expectant couple can seem so golden compared with what seems to be a grey and even desolate one for the childless. To their distress and perhaps guilt, an infertile couple can thus feel a gulf dividing them from those they love the most.

It is interesting that personally I have found that the joyful news of new pregnancies often reaches me at just two points. Sometimes it is when I am already very down, struggling badly, perhaps at the 'wrong' time of the month. Then it further intensifies the depression. But at other times, it comes just when I have perhaps gained a measure of victory over the pain in the preceding weeks. Maybe I have just been encouraged by an amazingly relevant Bible reading, or by a friend. Then such news has the power to knock me down and reverse the peace I had found. It can feel like a slap in the face, just when my head had risen above water again. The devil really does attempt to unseat us, and this issue is obviously one of the weakest chinks in my armour. I am sure the devil will also be doing his utmost to cause division and awkwardness between Christian brothers and sisters. We know we need to resist him.

It can be extremely hard to hear or know about those who fall pregnant and who were not expecting it so soon (or so late) in their lives and do not feel able to cope. It is more painful still to hear or know of others who really do not want their children at all, or who are not capable of caring for them properly or loving them when they are born. It is particularly awful for infertile people to watch media reports of children who have been neglected and abused; indeed, the infertile couple can feel almost insulted by such a situation. In contrast to the circumstances just observed, they, the childless ones, feel emotionally, physically and spiritually prepared to become parents. They have a home ready, and so much love waiting to offer a baby. So why does a baby not come to them instead? Life in this regard can just seem so desperately unfair.

It is not that the childless couple actually want someone else's baby. It is not necessarily that they refuse, point blank, to 'rejoice with those who rejoice'. They may be trying very hard to do this, to be gracious and big-hearted in their response. It is not that they do not care about the expectant couple, or want to be involved in their lives any more. It is certainly not that they wish them ill. It is just that any new pregnancy, no matter who the expectant couple are, is an unavoidable constant and visible reminder of all that the childless couple would so love to enjoy but do not have themselves. They might be truly happy for the couple concerned, and desperate that all will go well for them. But they may also be trying to cope with a bewildering combination of anger, hurtful thoughts, jealousy, hopelessness and feelings of injustice. They may be struggling with guilt about this, and attempting to bring all of these negative emotions under the control of the Holy Spirit. They need much prayer and support at this time.

It really does help if the expectant couple are sensitive and bear with their infertile friends here, not being offended if the childless couple do not always feel able to see them. The expectant couple themselves are likely to feel upset and awkward about the situation, but will almost certainly not be experiencing the distress and hopelessness of their childless friends.

Nick and I have known some dear couples struggle with childlessness but then happily become pregnant. Sometimes they are people with whom we have sympathized and prayed, and perhaps in whom we had found some mutual support. Yet now, as with all first-time parents, they have moved into a new realm, and we have been left behind. An infertile couple can still struggle with this. They will no doubt on the one hand be delighted for the couple, and some may even be caused to feel a little hopeful again themselves. But now that these friends are no longer 'one of us', they may also feel even more isolated, even a bit betrayed. However, despite all of this, Nick and I are thankful to the Lord that some of the most touching and deeply concerned letters we have received telling us of a new pregnancy have been from such friends: those who truly understand the pain. We are thankful that our friendships have continued, and we have been blessed through them.

Many childless couples will try to put on a brave face for the sake of new parents. Nick and I have always tried to be positive and joyful whenever a new baby is born to friends, relatives or church family. It can feel almost impossible at times, but God has enabled us to buy gifts and chat to new parents about their experiences. After all, the birth of a new baby *is* a truly wonderful blessing to the world. Obviously we do need babies to be born, especially into loving families, and of course we are hugely relieved when the babies arrive safe and well. Nevertheless, there have been times when I have been caught out in a 'baby' shop and have had to dash to the cloakrooms for a cry; or when I have returned home after time spent with a new baby and mother, or have just heard news of another pregnancy, and have yet again cried myself to sleep. We cry because it is never the joyful news of *our* baby, and I have often felt deeply sad that I cannot hear the announcement of a new pregnancy or birth, even concerning families whom I love very much, without struggling through this distressing mix of emotions.

Feelings of frustration and deficiency

Even if an infertile man or woman is blessed to be greatly involved in the lives of other people's children, there are painful reminders that they are not the parents, nor ever will be. As Katherine Hall describes it, there may be 'a genuine bond of love, but there can never be any sense of belonging, since each child has "Return to Owner" clearly stamped upon it'.[6] A childless friend, auntie or uncle may have been happily playing games with a little one of whom they are very fond and even love. But if something should go wrong, often it is only Mum who will do. At the end of the day, they always go back to Mum and Dad. We all know the unique place a mother has in her child's life. We can say exactly the same for fathers, and this is good, of course. But the gulf remains. Someone kindly suggested to one friend, 'Perhaps this is your role—to give weekend breaks to parents by looking after *their* children!' But this hurt my friend, as it was a reminder, yet again, of her own lack.

Some feel that a major part of their creativity is being stifled and that it may never flourish in any other way. Both Nick and I were blessed to grow up in loving, devoted families, and we have good relationships with our own parents. We have longed to establish such a family ourselves and pass on happy traditions, as well as the blessed spiritual heritage of knowing God. So we are frustrated and lack fulfilment at a deep level. Some couples, in feeling this sense of deficiency, become very restless, propelled to keep moving churches, homes or jobs: anything in an attempt to fill the aching void. And yet despite all this, nothing truly fills that gap. Permanently low spirits can set in. Sometimes as the years have passed I wonder, 'Whatever has happened to me? Where now is my sense of fun? Has my sense of adventure evaporated? Will it ever come back?' I have so often felt utterly exhausted by the emotional and spiritual impact of infertility.

Also, as a couple in ministry, Nick and I have often felt how helpful it would be to experience and understand parenting first-hand. When looking for a church in which to serve, we were aware that some churches especially seek pastors who have children. It was hard not to feel even more inadequate in our already painful and undesired situation.

Please remember any infertile couples you may know who are in some form of Christian ministry. Some will keenly feel their lack of practical experience with family issues when helping their congregations, and sometimes even in preparing sermons. Nick has struggled with this over the years. Those who are pastors may be the ones to announce the happy arrival of new church babies and lead in prayer for them and their families from the pulpit. They will likely be the ones to lead a christening, thanksgiving or dedication service. Their wives will be seeking to visit, congratulate, give gifts and listen to the new mums. They may feel they should not stay away from the baby showers, even if their feelings tell them they cannot face it yet another time (I stayed away once, soon after my miscarriage, and sent on a gift for the box with a friend; it was very graciously received).

The pastor and his wife do not have the option of staying away from church for long time periods when struggling with infertility. Most ministry couples will not begrudge any of the above, as they love their congregations and want to serve them. Hopefully they will know the Holy Spirit's strength and will still be able to impart helpful biblical wisdom to families. But it can be so hard when your own heart is broken. The infertile pastor and wife are just as human and sensitive as any other childless couple, and they are always in the public eye, which can be a strain when facing tragedy. They may be looked up to, and they may even be very godly, but they are certainly not superhero Christians!

Sadly I have realized in myself over the last few years a tendency to pull away somewhat from too much contact with babies and very young children. They often cry when I hold them, and I can feel self-conscious, aware of my lack of experience, and think, perhaps incorrectly, that people watching are feeling sorry for me. Sometimes it just hurts too much. I do feel grieved about this, when I think of how I used to adore other people's little ones when I was younger. I hope and trust that one day this may become easier again.

Identity crisis

The infertile woman who had hoped to raise children as her primary role in life may sense she is approaching something akin to a mid-life crisis. Perhaps she had hoped to find her main identity, as I had hoped for myself, in being the happy, secure and devoted mother of several children (or at least one child). This is probably more the case with women than with men, who, it appears, often find their sense of identity through their employment. If a childless woman has always envisaged society perceiving her primarily as a mother, what will 'define' her now?

Without exception, all the infertile women who have shared their stories for this book are attractive, intelligent and talented. But for most of them, the inability to conceive seems to eclipse many other 'achievements' they have attained so far in life. These now seem insignificant compared with that of raising a family. Any other work the infertile woman is doing may now seem less important to her than being a mother. What is she to be now? Who is she now? Perhaps she thinks, 'Isn't it a woman's *raison d'être* to bear and raise children? What is to be my purpose now?' She might begin to feel worthless. Some might bury themselves in their work or other occupations, hoping that this will give them a sense of understanding of why they were put on this earth. Others simply do not know what to do, especially if they are also in jobs where they are unhappy. How do they begin again? It is not easy to turn your thoughts to starting anew when all you still long for is to be a mother. With some such infertile women, regret starts to surface over previous life choices and missed opportunities. Has she somehow ignored something else she really should have been doing? Is it too late now?

Anticipating a bleak future

Many infertile couples will fear for the years that lie ahead, wondering how things will be for them in old age. While we may be getting older, and (for women) by our mid- to late-forties losing our potential to conceive, yet in these modern days of longevity we may still have half of our life ahead of us! But it will not perhaps be the life of which we dreamed. I have often considered this, truly wondering how I will cope.

This can be especially concerning for a childless couple if they do not have much other family around and envisage a time when they have lost their spouse and are completely alone, without the comfort and distraction of their children. Infertile couples realize that without the blessing of children, neither will they have grandchildren, noticing that many older people seem to find a new lease of life, with renewed joy and purpose, when they become grandparents. Will they be those who sit alone, week after week, in their increasing infirmity? It is hard for me to forget the anguish of one older infertile friend: she and her husband were well past childbearing age when her mother died. She confessed how nobody around her understood just how much her grief was compounded by her never having had any children of her own.

A long-term struggle with all of the above can leave a couple deeply discouraged, losing their social and self-confidence and even all hope for the future. Some will wonder what they have to live for if they cannot have children. Sometimes I still struggle with getting up in the morning, feeling that I have little to get up for. I usually become far more positive as the day proceeds (actually, I have lots to live for!), but on a bad day the future can seem so bleak and joyless, even empty. As one friend remembered, 'I felt we *had* no future.' Rachel, in the book of Genesis, watched her sister and maidservants easily conceive one child after another and cried out to her husband, 'Give me children, or I'll die!' We know that relationships were far from ideal in Jacob's household, and Rachel herself was struggling with jealousy and bitterness; but I am sure that many infertile women profoundly relate to that cry of despair. Indeed, suicidal thoughts are not uncommon.

Pause for thought

- Where are you in the grieving process?
- What is God saying to *you* at the moment?
- Write down three suggestions to help you cope on a difficult day.

Bible passages for reflection

Trust in him at all times, O people;
pour out your hearts to him,
for God is our refuge. (Ps. 62:8)

In bringing many sons to glory, it was fitting that God, for whom and through whom everything exists, should make the author of their salvation perfect through suffering … Because he himself suffered when he was tempted, he is able to help those who are being tempted. (Heb. 2:10, 18)

For we do not have a high priest who is unable to sympathize with our weaknesses, but we have one who has been tempted in every way, just as we are—yet was without sin. Let us then approach the throne of grace with confidence, so that we may receive mercy and find grace to help us in our time of need. (Heb. 4:15–16)

Prayer

Loving heavenly Father, you are the all-knowing and all-seeing God. You know my heart. You are keenly aware of everything I feel. You see all the pain and suffering inside. You know what no one else can know, of how much I ache. Father, it hurts so much. Please help me. Send your comforting Spirit to wrap me in the comfort you alone can give and that I so need.

Father, you know how I struggle to rejoice with those who rejoice over their own pregnancies and children. Please keep me from bitterness towards them. Keep me from envy. Give me a godly response. Thank you so much for Jesus, for One who identifies with me in suffering and who understands my pain and my temptations. Lord Jesus, when my trauma is so great, and I feel so numb I can scarcely pray, please pray for me with the depth of understanding that you alone have. Amen.

Social angst

Isolation

If a couple do not feel able to share their situation with anyone else they may feel very isolated. But even Nick and I, in our openness about our experience, can still feel very cut off, particularly in general terms, from our peer group. If we had been given the blessing of a baby when we first started trying (as many are), our child would, at the time of writing, now be over eleven years old. Sometimes I see mothers waiting at the school gate, happily chatting with each other. I often think they look about my age and that I would like to befriend them. Other women make lots of new friends through Mother and Toddler groups. Yet without children I have no natural point of contact with them.

Most of the women I know who are having their first child are now at least ten years younger than me, and many of them are much younger still. Landmark thirtieth and fortieth birthdays can be painful for those of us who have not yet had any children. The children of our siblings and friends are growing up fast: some of them are in their mid-teens now. Sometimes I have looked in the mirror, and on spotting a new grey hair or wrinkle have thought, 'I am getting older … and I am *still* not a mother!' I recently heard how a young girl whom I taught in the Infants class sixteen years ago is now married and a mother. Such news yet again seems to emphasize that time is quickly passing me by, and my dreams are fast becoming out of reach. It can almost feel that there is a 'club' to which we, as infertile people, do not belong. We can feel a bit 'abnormal'. These feelings can be so strong that it sometimes surprises me when people ask me if I have children. I think, 'Surely it's obvious that I am not a mother? Can't you tell? Don't I seem something of a social outsider, perhaps immature or inexperienced? Doesn't it show in my face, in my behaviour?'

As described before, one major problem of infertility is our perception that not many others understand the tremendous pain. Although the numbers of couples with these issues are on the increase, we are still relatively few. We can feel that we, and we alone, have been singled out for this pain. And this can be incredibly isolating.

Pressure from society

The apparent modern Western obsession with having children to gain self-fulfilment can have a negative knock-on effect for infertile couples. It is very difficult to hear or read comments like, 'I knew I could never be happy unless I had a child, and I have never felt so fulfilled by anything else in all my life ... Having a baby has made my life complete!' The infertile couple may also feel that for them, humanly speaking, nothing else could ever be so exciting or precious as a positive pregnancy test followed by the birth of their own child. We seem to hear and read so much of this in the media. Many couples will indeed declare that the most amazing moment in their life has been the birth of their first child. But the infertile couple may never experience any of this. Books, radio, TV and even adverts do not let us forget our infertility. There seems to be an overflow of articles or discussions about conception, pregnancy and parenting. Some of them can be hurtful or even insulting. I once read an article in a (quality) newspaper which seemed to be suggesting that fertile women are also more physically beautiful than their infertile peers. One can only guess the effect this would have at breakfast time on a woman who yet again cried herself to sleep the night before.

The fact is that most people *do* have children, and it often seems that our society is geared around families and their needs. A few friends have suggested that one major division in society may be between those who have children and those who do not. Many people in social gatherings talk at great length about their children and grandchildren. They may not realize how much they are doing this, as their families are an obvious source of delight and blessing to them. But the childless couple, and also perhaps those who are not grandparents but would love to be, can feel very insignificant during such conversations. They have to find other things to converse about with people (and to write about in the Christmas 'round robin' letters). At least a couple of young mothers have confessed to me that in some socially difficult situations they 'hide behind their children', or sit with them if there is no one else to sit with. Obviously, a childless woman does not have this advantage! A couple with children who move to a new neighbourhood will often find it easier to befriend new people, as their children become a natural contact point with others, playing with the neighbours' kids, or, as I have noted already, enabling them to meet other parents at the school gate. A childless couple may need to be a bit more creative and put in more work to make new friends.

Some childless people are caused to wonder if their family and friends would love them more if they had children, or at least if such a happy and shared experience would bond them all closer together. Some fertile couples have spoken of how a new baby became a 'healer' in a difficult family situation. Perhaps the infertile couple had really wanted their parents to know the joy of having grandchildren; but this may not happen now—at least, not through them.

Similarly, while most people would guess that unhappily *single* people may find social occasions such as weddings hard, they may not realize that infertile couples can do too. At a wedding there can be many reminders for them of their own situation. For example, many forms of the Christian marriage service include something about producing children; sometimes it is the first reason mentioned as to why God designed marriage. Our wedding service even contained the blessing in a prayer, 'Have many children'(!). Sometimes prospective children are made much of in the reception speeches. This is, of course, all very natural and usually good. But an infertile couple may look back with great poignancy to their own wedding day, which for them too had included the joyful hope of having their own children. It may cause them to wonder yet again if God has given their partnership His blessing after all. Those who have been struggling with infertility for a long time may consider rather ruefully that this newly married couple will probably have children before they do (and for us this is now usually the case).

Some of the ways in which God has helped us in our emotional and social struggles can be found in Chapters 10, 11, 12 and 13.

Pause for thought

- What are you doing to create social contacts?
- Would making contact with other Christian couples in your situation be helpful for you?
- Write a list of three tips you might give another couple to help them cope with the difficult social situations that arise.

Bible passages for reflection

... Do not fear, for I am with you;
  do not be dismayed, for I am your God.
I will strengthen you and help you;
  I will uphold you with my righteous right hand. (Isa. 41:10)

I know what it is to be in need, and I know what it is to have plenty. I have learned the secret of being content in any and every situation, whether well fed or hungry, whether living in plenty or in want. I can do everything through him who gives me strength. (Phil. 4:12–13)

Prayer

Gracious Father, you are the Giver of many good gifts. All that we have comes from you. When I look at the society around me I see that many people find great pleasure and joy in their children. Father, you know how that makes me feel at times. You know how I can feel abnormal, missing out on something that is so much part of normal human existence. Yet I know you have given me so much already. Please help me to be truly grateful for what I have, and grant me contentment. Above all, help me not to seek pleasure and fulfilment in material things, or even in children, but in you alone. In the name of Jesus, Amen.

Marriage problems

Tension

As with other bereavements, a couple may struggle because they do not both respond to this grief in the same way or with the same intensity. As described in the Preface, Nick is certain that our situation has, in general, been more painful for me than for him; he has admitted finding it difficult to fully understand all my feelings. He confesses how it occasionally appeared that his words spoken with lack of understanding missed the mark. Admittedly, in the depths of my grief, my reactions to Nick's loving and diligent attempts to help were not always very gracious. The trauma should have drawn us only closer together, as we wept together. But the different degrees to which it impacted us could have threatened to drive us apart. Nick admits that at times he felt perplexed and anxious about my spiritual and emotional struggles, and about his ability to help.

Perhaps most women will struggle more acutely than their husbands, but this is not always so. With us, the sadness of our situation has affected Nick and me in different ways over the years. I have struggled intensely from the beginning of this trial, with many periods of ups and downs. My personality tends towards pessimism, and on receiving our first diagnosis I realized very quickly and clearly what implications infertility would have for us: the ramifications we would struggle against. By contrast, Nick is more of an optimist; but, he admits, sometimes unrealistically so. At the beginning, when I was cast into the depths of despair, he was still full of hope about our situation. Nick has found that his sorrow and sadness increase as we get older, as the years roll on and as his sense of hope in the situation fades. This has been especially the case since our miscarriage, when the pregnancy had fuelled his desire for a child. He now considers that his coping mechanism may have initially been strong because he originally saw our infertility as only a temporary problem. He wonders whether he may struggle more as time goes by and the menopause approaches, while perhaps I may be coping better by then.

As yet, we have been blessed with a good marriage, and although our heartache over childlessness has caused some great tensions and pain, and while we do have these very different personality types, thankfully it has not resulted in any deeply divisive problems for us so far. We pray much that this may remain so. This is not the case for everybody, though. How do a couple cope with a situation of infertility if they cannot understand each other's feelings at all, when each is swamped by their own personal grief? Each of us is unique, and sometimes a disparity in emotional response to this hard trial can lead to a huge gulf dividing husbands and wives. This may be widened because they also differ markedly in how they want to remedy the situation, perhaps over treatment options, how they spend their money concerning it, or over adoption. One spouse may be far keener than the other to explore and take up these possibilities.

Physical and emotional struggles

Life can be especially tough for couples following a fertility programme, when every waking moment seems to be dominated by it. If a woman is using hormone treatment, her emotions are likely to be far more unstable than usual, and she really needs much sympathy and patience. Temptations to chronic moaning, temper outbursts and grinding negativity are not unusual in these circumstances, compounding the existing tensions. Any pre-existing physical difficulties and tiredness may become much more acute. Yet if her husband is battling through his own feelings about it all he may not find he is able to help her much. Furthermore, infertility can eventually take its toll on the intimate life of a couple: it can become strained and weary. Sex is naturally so bound up in the creation of new life (although as a society we have rather successfully managed to forget that fact until we *want* to have children). But when a baby does not come along for months or more, this side of marriage can become a focus for that failure. It can be so disheartening. On the other hand, it can also easily become just a means to an end: the desired 'end' of a baby. Checking the monthly calendar for the optimum 'conception days' can definitely take the spontaneity out of it all! Some medical intervention sidesteps sex altogether during treatment programmes, divorcing it from the whole situation. For some couples, this can intensify an atmosphere of unreality.

It is not always easy to live together when there is depression, disappointment, spiritual struggles and anger to deal with. A couple may also be suffering great pressures from outside, perhaps from family members. They may then be tempted to blame each other for insensitive comments from each other's family. Sometimes there is the temptation to blame each other for the entire situation. This may be especially so if the previous lifestyle choices of one spouse have actually resulted in the difficulties (tragically, abortions and certain sexually transmitted diseases can sometimes result in complications leading to infertility and miscarriage). All couples struggling with any of the above issues need much prayer and support. They may also need to be honest with God and ask for more of His help.

The need for a fruitful marriage

As described before, many Christian couples do regard physical fruitfulness in their marriage as a mark of God's blessing and therefore as a sign of its 'rightness'. They desire to produce a child who is part of them both, who will perhaps resemble each of them in many ways. Consider Adam, who on fathering Seth was evidently considered blessed to have been given 'a son in his own likeness, in his own image' (Gen. 5:3). Katherine Hall, in *Learning to Cope with Childlessness*, makes a very interesting point about marital fruitfulness. When Hannah prayed to God in desperation for a son (1 Sam. 1), she also promised to give him to the Lord from an early age. So after Samuel was weaned, he went to live permanently at the temple in Shiloh. Some may wonder, what was the point of Hannah longing for a child, if she was then to give him up? Katherine Hall suggests,

> The answer presumably lies in the God-given need of a husband and wife for fulfilment in their marriage, for the child who sets the seal on their union and renders it fruitful. Even if the child Samuel's parents hardly saw him again, he was indubitably there, the object of love and prayer and thought even in his absence. He was the focus for their marriage.[1]

So where does that leave a couple if such 'fruit' and focus is absent—when the ‘quiver’ is ‘empty’? Should they perhaps not have married in the first place? Some couples will be painfully aware from their medical diagnoses that if one (or both) of them had married other partners, they probably would be parents. Even though Nick and I have unexplained fertility issues, in the past I have often been tempted to think that if Nick had married someone else, he might be a father by now because the ‘problem’ is perhaps more likely to be with me. This of course may not be the case; it could be an undetectable problem with Nick, or indeed with us both. But we can see how such problems could lead to deep rifts in a marriage.

It is interesting that Hannah’s response to Elkanah’s (seemingly insensitive) question, ‘Don’t I mean more to you than ten sons?’ is not recorded in Scripture for us. Elkanah was almost certainly trying to encourage Hannah, the wife whom he loved so much. But, as in any tragic and difficult situation within marriage, we do not always respond helpfully to each other. Tragically, some couples do finally find themselves drifting into separation and divorce, their marriages irrevocably torn apart under the heart-rending trials of infertility.

Some of the ways God has helped us specifically in our marriage can be found in Chapters 9 and 11.

Pause for thought

- How would you describe the personality differences between you and your spouse?
- How have these differences affected the way you have responded to infertility?
- Write down three things you are going to do in the next month to keep building your marriage.
- Write a prayer for your current situation.

Bible passages for reflection

Each one of you also must love his wife as he loves himself, and the wife must respect her husband. (Eph. 5:33)

Husbands ... be considerate as you live with your wives, and treat them with respect as the weaker partner and as heirs with you of the gracious gift of life, so that nothing will hinder your prayers. (1 Peter 3:7)

'In your anger do not sin': Do not let the sun go down while you are still angry, and do not give the devil a foothold. (Eph. 4:26–27)

Prayer

God of the covenant, you bound yourself to your people with an undying love. Your covenant love and faithfulness endure for ever. You will never forsake us. Thank you so much for the marriage partner you have given me, and for bringing us together in a similar covenant. Father, you know how much our suffering has impacted our marriage. You know the tensions we have. You've witnessed our arguments, our hurtful and unkind comments. You've seen into our hearts. Merciful Father, please forgive us. Please help us to work through this together. We're aware that marriages have broken down because of the impact of such problems. Please give us grace to keep the covenant we've made with each other. Strengthen our marriage. For your glory's sake, Amen.

Chapter 5

Medical issues

Dealing with the medical side of infertility can be a varied experience, differing enormously from couple to couple. Some are thankfully blessed with a very positive situation overall. They have encountered helpful, caring hospital staff and been given a clear, simple diagnosis, by means of which the problem can be remedied with relative ease. Their treatment has progressed smoothly, and finally they become the parents they had so longed to be. If only this could be the case for every hurting couple! Many others meet with a few setbacks along the way, but eventually pull through with a happy outcome. Sadly, though, for some, beginning medical intervention can be the start of an uncertain, complex or even traumatic journey in itself, which may not ever result in the joy of a child being safely born. Regardless of how positive or otherwise a couple's experience of fertility treatment is, there is still not yet a 100 per cent success rate for any programme.

Due to the potential difficulties involved, some couples attempting to conceive do not wish to go to the doctor or have any diagnosis made of their condition at all. They might feel they cannot face the invasion of their privacy or the trauma of an unpleasant outcome. There is good reason to be wary and prepared, for some tests and procedures may drag on with great intensity and uncertainty for weeks, months or even longer. In addition, certain diagnoses of infertility can open up a minefield of difficult choices for a couple. They may have to make decisions about things they had hoped they would never have to think about.

Facing possible humiliation and distress

Most doctors seem to be busy and stretched to full capacity; they are doing their best but have so many patients on their books. I am certain most of them are very concerned for the infertile couples in their care. We ourselves have discovered this to be so, much of the time. Despite this, infertility medical investigations can be very disheartening. Couples may have deeply personal aspects of their private life together opened up for discussion with specialist medical staff who are sometimes unsympathetic. The couple may not always feel they are really being cared for or understood as individuals: perhaps they are just another couple on a factory belt of tests and procedures. Worse than this, though, Nick and I have actually had our pro-life concerns refused consideration and our pro-biblical views of sex disbelieved and mocked to our faces by one NHS consultant, who also made clumsy jokes at our expense.

Both husband and wife may have to submit to tests which they find unpleasant and embarrassing. Some Christian men have admitted to being deeply dismayed by the immoral nature of some 'reading' material presented to them at clinics when producing samples for investigation. The infertile woman in particular may have to face a barrage of physically invasive, painful and even humiliating procedures. A women's reproductive system is very complex and delicate, more than that of a man, and there is so much that can be wrong. She may well be left feeling that she is no more than a physical body with precious little dignity. Some of these tests may be done under general anaesthetic, and there will be others too when her husband cannot be with her. And no matter how skilled, caring and knowledgeable the team of doctors may be, procedures can still sometimes go wrong.

Unfortunately, the manner in which test results are given can also sometimes be less than sensitive. One friend recalls how she woke up after a major diagnostic operation. Half an hour later she was still feeling groggy and vulnerable because her husband was not with her. But it was at that point a doctor sat down on her bed and told her outright that the results of her tests were so negative she would probably never have children. When Nick and I were given our first devastating diagnosis in 2001, the registrar could only guess at what might have caused such a hopeless situation. He actually wrote his suggestion on my medical records, despite our protestations; we knew this could not be correct. Our second laparoscopy overturned his 'guess', and a simple blood test conducted years later dispelled any doctor's doubts that we were right. Are this registrar's original comments still on my medical records? We don't know. Hopefully, they have been amended.

But it was all very distressing, and it shows how couples can sometimes feel out of control during the whole investigative procedure.

Even after enduring many months of testing, some couples (like ourselves) still find to their frustration that there is no clear diagnosis. As mentioned before, despite vastly advanced technological methods there is still plenty that the doctors do not know about infertility. On the other hand, a bleak prognosis can be devastating to couples who had lived for years not realizing there was anything wrong with them. We can feel somehow betrayed by our own bodies. One friend disclosed that the totally unexpected and utterly hopeless results of their fertility investigations left her so traumatized she needed tranquillizers. I remember being so nervous when attending our second major consultation that I needed physical support to walk into the hospital.

Feeling like physical failures

It really does seem that in our world one of the most basic aspects of being male and female is to be seen to be able to procreate. Many women do have a very strong biological and physical urge to conceive, bear and nurture their own child, and this is surely the way God made us. The knowledge that our biological clock is ticking away but that nothing is happening, and perhaps there is little help available, can produce feelings of panic. Being physically unable to conceive and bear children can produce an enormously deep sense of inadequacy. Infertile women know that they are missing out on an experience which is a very natural part of being female. Conceiving a baby, experiencing the enormous physical and mental changes pregnancy brings, feeling the child move inside, seeing it grow, giving birth and breastfeeding are sometimes seen as a normal 'rite of passage' for women. I have often struggled with feeling that I am not a 'proper' woman because my body cannot seem to do what a woman's body was designed and created for.

'Masculinity' too can so often be unhelpfully linked with fatherhood in popular thought and jesting. Even Jacob in Genesis 49:3 declared that Reuben, his oldest child and son, was the 'first sign of [his] strength'. Such ideas still abound today. Where does that leave an infertile man? Although we know that infertile men are no less physically strong and masculine than their fertile counterparts, there are many who feel utterly brought down by a negative diagnosis on their part. Some may never wish to admit the problem or discuss it with anyone, whether the cause is genetic, accidental, or due to earlier medical problems (such as mumps). Some, quite understandably, will not want their wives to talk about it either, but this can be desperately isolating for such women. Years ago I read the poignant biography of an Oxfordshire shepherd. 'Old Mont' lost his adored fiancée in tragic circumstances shortly after the First World War. Six years later, he had an appalling accident which left him incapable of ever fathering children. Mont never married after that. He finally opened up to a female journalist writing his life story in 1986, 'I were that destroyed. I never told a soul in my life till now; not even our Mam. There were only one I could have suffered to have shared such a shameful secret. [Thankfully] her were at peace in the Vale of Evesham and never lived to have to bear the burden of it.'[1]

The book *Just the Two of Us?* has a very helpful chapter with testimonies from Christian men who are struggling to accept their infertility.

Confusion over the whole situation

It can be deeply frustrating and very perplexing for the infertile couple who, as far as possible, take great care of themselves, physically and mentally, when they see others falling pregnant with ease who do not seem to care for themselves much at all. Infertile couples often feel very vulnerable, and it is so easy to become consumed by the situation. Even if they are not actually undergoing treatment, they may still constantly worry about dates and temperatures for optimum conception. They may read all they can, trying numerous expensive therapies, relaxation/exercise routines and special diets; their trolleys may be the healthiest in the supermarket every week, and yet sadly for them it makes no difference to their situation at all.

I have found this to be particularly so with us in our unexplained infertility. Because there is nothing definitely diagnosed as wrong, I am often wondering if it is caused by something I have done or am doing to myself. It is tempting to try solving any possible problem in any suggested way. But it is always just a shot in the dark. How do I know what will make the difference? One couple will be adamant they conceived through a therapy; another, through medical intervention; another, through counselling; still others, through eventually managing to relax despite everything. Why is it so different in each case, and what course do we pursue, if any? Why does

God seem to work in such diverse ways to bring children into the world? Would they have been conceived anyway, regardless of what the parents did or did not do? We may never know the answers to these questions in this life.

Recently I read a new book which, although interesting and helpful in many respects, also advocated a total organic and vegan diet to maximize chances of conception and to delay menopause. It listed a number of very ordinary foods (some of which are actually considered healthy) that the author believes may impede fertility. Later I heard on the radio that couples living in polluted urban areas are more likely to experience miscarriage. How can we know whether this advice is correct or not? Adhering to such a diet and moving to the countryside are not viable options for Nick and me—at the moment anyway. Yet hearing information of this nature can make infertile couples very unsettled, even guilt-stricken, that perhaps they are just not doing enough; or worse, that they are even unwittingly harming their fertility. Of course, adding to all the confusion is the constant reminder that most other couples seem to conceive without considering any of this.

The reverse of the problem can be for those who have been given a permanently negative prognosis. There may then be the temptation to simply give up caring for themselves at all, because what is the point?

Anguished choices over treatment options

Sadly, there are certain diagnoses of infertility for which medical help is still currently unavailable. Other couples are considered unfit to receive treatment for various reasons, such as emotional or mental instability. This in itself will obviously be very distressing for them. However, as medical technology advances, most couples are now presented with an increasing number of fertility programme options. While we are amazed about and thankful for much that can be done today, we cannot ignore the fact that some of these treatments are very physically invasive, highly complex and increasingly questionable in their ethics. Some may possibly be physically or emotionally harmful in the long term. A couple will have to read and sign a thick pile of consent forms, and consider carefully if there are aspects to the treatment they would not be happy with. We discovered that the negative aspects of certain options on the NHS were not always mentioned in the preliminary information packs (often they were only in the small print elsewhere) or discussed by our gynaecology teams.

Some couples will disagree with certain medical options presented to them on moral, ethical or biblical grounds. They may well withdraw from any treatment that creates and then destroys or experiments on embryos, or which involves the use of cloning or of donor gametes from a third party (outside their marriage), or which employs a surrogate.

Indeed, with some treatment options there will be certain delicate considerations for the couple to discuss together—issues which many of us would really rather not think through, as they are very emotive. But Nick and I are convinced they need to be well thought out, especially before the couple become too emotionally bound up in hope about any planned procedure. For example, if a couple opt for standard IVF, they must be aware that, although doctors may aim to produce multiple embryos from one treatment cycle, these days they will usually implant only one or two embryos at a time. If the others are considered to be in 'good' condition they may be frozen and kept for any future cycles. If not, they will be destroyed. If a couple opt for 'natural' IVF, the use of fertility drugs is minimal, and often only one embryo will be created. But if this one is found to be less than 'perfect', most doctors conducting the treatment would hesitate or even refuse to proceed with implantation in that tragic circumstance. Couples will also need to decide (and sign an agreement about) what would happen to their newly created life in the unlikely, but still possible, event that one or both of them died in the few days between fertilization and implantation, as they will go home from the hospital during this period.

It is truly distressing to consider such awful possibilities. This is especially so for those Christians who believe the Bible teaches that life begins at conception and so may then regard any treatment employing such procedures as not an option for them. This may nonetheless be utterly devastating to some who have been told that for them there are no other treatment options. That is exactly the position Nick and I found ourselves in during the time of our initial infertility diagnosis. Indeed, the necessity of considering all the above dilemmas left me feeling faint and sick, and needing to leave the hospital, our 'consent' forms forever unsigned. At that time it seemed that we were permanently closing the door to any possibility of the family we longed for.

Some couples known to us felt pressurized, from various directions, into following a certain course of treatment which they did not fully understand or felt unready to face. The treatment options are naturally presented to couples at a time when they are struggling badly, usually in the aftermath of a negative diagnosis. Some are perhaps still in shock, and yet the desperation to become parents is at a peak of intensity. They are likely to feel very defenceless. One friend recalls a conversation about the ethics of her treatment options with a fertility nurse. She says, 'When I said that I had some ethical problems with one of the major treatments available the nurse asked me what my religion was. I said that I was an evangelical Christian, but that I also knew that some other religious groups would not feel comfortable with it either, especially in light of the new camera technology and the TV programmes about conception. She patronizingly responded, "But they all have it in the end though, you know."'

Some treatment programmes, particularly if they are re-attempted due to repeated failure, can expend much time, masses of emotional energy and huge amounts of money. For all of these reasons, and as mentioned before, undergoing any fertility programme can cause added and acute stress to a couple's marriage. If the treatment involves much more focus on one partner (most likely the woman), the other (usually the man) may be left resentfully feeling they are little more than an accessory to the proceedings. Each couple will somehow have to assess all the options available to them and make a choice about how to proceed, if at all. They need much in the way of compassionate support and informed advice, but some find that to be sadly lacking.

The pain of treatment failing

It is very difficult for many infertile couples to accept that, for them, having a baby may only come 'unnaturally', and even at a high price. They may indeed feel that what should be so normal, straightforward and yet precious has become reduced to a mere scientific process. Nevertheless, many childless couples longing for a baby cope bravely with many awkward, time-consuming, unpleasant or painful procedures just to have the blessing of their own child. Indeed, hearing the wonderful success stories of some couples on assisted conception techniques can be a spur to others. We ourselves know of many such couples whose various different treatments have happily resulted in the family they longed for. Yet caution needs to be exercised because for others, of course, the treatments fail. If too much hope has been invested in them, there will be many shattered pieces to pick up afterwards. Some couples pursue a treatment option several times, but each time ends in failure. I was very struck by one couple's description of how they were *assured* by their medical staff that a certain lengthy and expensive treatment would work for them. When it failed, Malcolm and Nick Cameron were left devastated. Nick reflects on her experience in their helpful book *It's OK to Cry*:

> So infertility treatment was for me a catalogue of hopes raised, intrusive procedures, various side effects, repeated disappointment and despair. I had pills, drugs, scans, injections and surgery. Countless men and women prodded and poked at me. At one time my arms and thighs were bruised for weeks because of the repeated blood tests and injections. I had really had enough! My emotions couldn't take it. My body couldn't take it, and it was doing my spiritual life no good at all.[2]

Travelling to the hospital, fulfilling appointments and following a meticulous programme can take up countless hours. One Christian fertility specialist we know considers the frustration of delayed appointments, repeated tests, seeing different doctors every time, conflicting advice, slow progress through the investigations and treatments, as well as NHS funding restraints to be real problems for those infertile couples she is involved with. Of course, if all of these efforts result in the much-wanted baby, it will all be more than worthwhile. But what if, as is also often the case, it does not work? This couple may then feel it all to have been futile; all of that effort, time, pain, emotional drain and perhaps money was for nothing. The spiritual waste of time may be keenly felt. They could have been spending time in more productive pursuits … anything other than continually traipsing up to the hospital and keeping appointments that ended in failure.

The pain of giving up medical intervention

Some couples discover that remaining faithful to their consciences regarding the ethics of certain fertility treatments may mean that they will need to refuse the option suggested for them. Humanly speaking, therefore, their chances of conceiving or giving birth may well be much lowered or diminished altogether. Such a refusal would also be going against the generally accepted practice of our culture as it is now, and may well be one of the biggest sacrifices that couple ever make. They need the greatest respect and support from others in such a decision.

Finally, most infertile couples undergoing unsuccessful and prolonged medical intervention eventually come to a point when they realize that it is time to stop. Some fear they are losing their rationality with the stress and disappointment of it all, and recognize the need to see that there can be life beyond infertility and endless hospital visits. For some, this decision may be something of a relief. But the finality of this decision in itself can also seem like an added bereavement. Again, Nick Cameron writes, 'Believe me, it was one of the most difficult choices that we have ever had to make.'[3]

Some of the ways God has specifically helped us through our medical traumas can be found in Chapter 8.

Pause for thought

- How are you feeling and thinking right now about the options available to you for fertility treatment?
- Do these choices feature too much or too little in your prayers?
- For you as a couple, what would 'life beyond fertility' look like?

Bible passages for reflection

My frame was not hidden from you
  when I was made in the secret place.
When I was woven together in the depths of the earth,
  your eyes saw my unformed body.
All the days ordained for me
  were written in your book
  before one of them came to be. (Ps. 139:15–16)

The LORD is my shepherd, I shall not be in want.
  He makes me lie down in green pastures,
he leads me beside quiet waters,
  he restores my soul.
He guides me in paths of righteousness
  for his name's sake.
Even though I walk
  through the valley of the shadow of death,
I will fear no evil,
  for you are with me;
your rod and your staff,
  they comfort me. (Ps. 23:1–4)

Prayer

Loving God, I know you have compassion for those suffering medically; you show us in the person of Jesus, as he healed multitudes. You have established the medical profession to help those with medical problems today. Thank you, Father. But you know how degrading and unpleasant it can be to go through all the various investigations and tests. You know how distressing and wearing it can be to have hopes raised, just to be dashed if treatment fails. Please strengthen us for all that we shall face. Go with us as our Shepherd to lead us, sustain us, comfort and protect us if we go through dark and difficult valleys. Give wisdom to the doctors as they examine, draw their conclusions, and try to help. Sovereign Lord, if your good and perfect plan is for us to remain childless, guide us as a couple to agree on when we should cease seeking medical help. If and when that day comes, please be our all-in-all. Amen.

Unhelpful responses from others

I have already described how it is utterly devastating for a couple to endure suggestions from others that their infertility is due to a lack of faith in God, or even because of sin. But sadly, there are many other ways in which people wound the childless. I know how careful we need to be here: I am now convinced that many of the unhelpful and even highly insensitive comments I have struggled with over the years have been made by those who do actually care very much and are trying to help. As I mentioned before, many people just do not know how to respond. The world of infertility is outside most people's experience. I think some are very uneasy with the awful possibility that things may never work out well for us in this trial. So they say almost anything, no matter how thoughtless or clumsy, in an effort to comfort or help.

When we have been hurt, the temptation can be to want to inflict pain back: to hurt others, perhaps by responding in a way that makes them embarrassed or uncomfortable because we ourselves are so hurt. But this is not Christlike. A struggling infertile couple may well need to find a coping strategy and avoid discussing problems with certain insensitive people. They will almost certainly need carefully to create standard answers with which they can fend off nosey and hurtful comments and so protect themselves. However, as Christians we do need to develop a forgiving and gracious spirit. It is not always easy to forget unbelievable rudeness (although some of it has been almost laughable anyway), but becoming bitter and keeping an up-to-date and forever-open record of wrongs will not help anyone in the end. Lois Flowers describes how we must not become oversensitive. If somebody is describing in highly excited detail how blessed they are with their children, or because their sixth grandchild has just been born, 99 times out of 100 it is not meant to be a jibe at the infertile listener. She urges us that we need to develop 'thick skins' while remaining 'soft-hearted' towards the hurts and needs of others. This can be a big challenge!

Furthermore, as another pastor's wife so wisely pointed out to me, there are many trials in life that I myself will never experience. I may therefore unknowingly hurt someone else who is struggling with a problem outside my own orbit. My attempts to help them may therefore be inappropriate or seem thoughtless. It is actually possible that Nick and I have also offended other childless people who are struggling with different aspects of the situation from us. Every infertile person is an individual, so perhaps we will each feel uniquely about what is unhelpful or hurtful. We all need God's constant help to forgive and be gracious when we are extremely hard-pressed.

So Nick and I want to emphasize that this chapter is not intended either to wallow in bitterness or to get back at any who may have said or done what was unhelpful for us. However, every infertile person I have spoken with has been the recipient of at least one hurtful comment, or has endured difficult or even very distressing encounters with others who showed little empathy regarding their situation. Many infertile people may therefore closely identify with what is recorded here. But if you are reading this book to try to grow in your understanding of your infertile friends, the following are many examples of unhelpful responses drawn from our own experiences, and from those of our friends, which might be best avoided.

Surviving intrusive questions and insensitive comments

Unfortunately, some people on the outside of an infertility situation do not seem to realize that questions like, 'Do you have any children?' followed immediately by, 'Oh? *How* long have you been married?', or, 'When are you going to get on with it? What are you waiting for? You're not getting any younger!' seem unkind and rude, especially when there are other people present and listening. I have even had such questions asked me in a holiday church setting, among people I hardly knew! Most of the infertile couples we know have had many such personal questions directed at them, and often in public or social situations.

Of course, an obvious topic of conversation on meeting a new acquaintance is to ask them if they have any children, but I have generally stopped asking that to others now. I assume that most people who have children will bring them into the conversation at some point anyway, as most people love talking about their children (and grandchildren). If they do not, perhaps there may be other reasons why they do not wish to discuss them. On a few occasions, this question being asked of me has led to some helpful and supportive conversations with sensitive people. But it is still always painful to be asked, and sadly some people will push the point. I once replied to the 'family' question like this: 'Yes, we have parents, siblings, nephews and a niece.' 'But do you have any *children*?' the person persisted. Some will even respond with quips such as, 'Oh, you should, it is just wonderful! Ours have brought us such joy!' Not a few of us infertile women have actually had our abdomens patted, even by people we do not know very well, with the question, 'So, when are you going to start a family, then?' Or, 'When are we going to hear the patter of tiny feet?' Even in a loving family situation, such (often jovial) questions can make an already distressed and anxious couple feel even more under pressure. With a supportive friend or family member there may be a place for such a question to be asked gently and seriously, in private and out of genuine concern. That would need to be judged depending on the closeness and trust already existing.

There have been times when I have revealed to a questioner that we are struggling to have children, perhaps on one of my 'stronger' days, hoping that would be the end of it. But then they have subjected me to a barrage of further questions: 'Oh, what is wrong with you?' Or, 'Have you had/why don't you have [a certain treatment]?' 'Have you ever thought of adopting? Or perhaps you could foster? If I were childless, that's what I would do!' being most common. I have even heard said to a man I did not know at a social gathering, 'Are you firing blanks?' I need say nothing about the first and last questions; sadly, even ruder ones have been directed at some couples, together with crude and cruel jokes. (I turn to the issue of adoption below.)

If I do not wish to discuss our childlessness at all, I usually respond briskly and lightly to the question with something like, 'No, we don't [have any children]—but do you?' Using this defence mechanism I can then usually direct the questions, asking them about their own families. My heart can glaze over a little and recover while I listen and move the conversation on. I have become quite adept at this over the years. (Nick sometimes responds to the 'Do you have children?' question by joking, 'No, we've been spared that trial!')

For me personally, the most helpful response to my negative reply about not having children is for the questioner to acknowledge my answer briefly and sensitively and then tactfully to change the subject. One good response might run something like this: 'Oh, I'm so sorry to hear that. It must be very hard for you. There's a lot in life that we don't understand, isn't there?' If it is said in genuine sympathy, I may take the conversation further. However, when I do reveal that Nick and I are, in fact, childless, the 'ice-breaker' social conversation usually terminates in an embarrassed silence. If I wish to revive it, I might then continue with all the cheerfulness I can muster—something like, 'But I love having nephews and nieces/my work!' Or again, I might ask them about their own families.

Some kind people say things like, 'It's such a shame. You would be wonderful parents.' I have often found this rather comforting, as in my blackest moments I have wondered if I have no children because I would be an unfit mother; but I know one man who does not like any such comments on his suitability. For him, it simply rubs salt into the wound. However, I have also (unbelievably) heard that some infertile people have been hit with such staggeringly callous suggestions as, 'Maybe God hasn't given you any children because you just wouldn't have been a very good mother/father ...' Surely the only answer to that can be, 'I don't *think* so!'—I am sure we can all recall examples, perhaps at least in the media, of men and women who are appalling parents and yet managed to conceive without a spot of bother.

Some people attempt to 'jolly things up' a little with a childless person they do not know well. However, quips such as, 'Well, at least you can have fun trying!' or, 'Oh well, it obviously just isn't meant to be!' are not especially helpful to most childless couples we know. This last remark, if delivered in such a way, can raise more questions than it answers. Others will suggest, 'Why don't you get a dog? They are a marvellous baby substitute!' Some people will say, 'What's the big problem? I never really wanted children, but ended up with them anyway!' Neither does it help us to hear about those who 'cannot understand infertility' because, by their own admission, they were so fertile that excessive preventative measures needed to be taken.

Sadly, these comments are just the tip of the iceberg.

Many childless couples have been told (usually by fertile people) that they are in an enviable position because they can go on exciting holidays, have more money to spend, and can pursue a career or hobbies, do what they like with their time and generally have a more relaxed life. This, of course, may sometimes be true, and we do have many good gifts to thank God for, as I will mention later. However, many infertile couples would gladly exchange numerous worldly pleasures for a child, and it is hollow comfort simply to suggest these things can in any way be a replacement for one.

Strange as it may seem, comments like, 'You are still looking so well/fit/young' immediately followed with, 'It must be because you don't have children!' rarely help anyone to be positive about childlessness. It is lovely to receive compliments, of course—but not to be then reminded glibly of what has caused such acute pain in our lives.

Others try to be helpful by suggesting, with various degrees of sensitivity, that we just pull our socks up and get on with life. After all, some people suffer 'much worse problems, take […], for example.' It is rarely helpful to have such comparisons forced upon us, as it can make us feel guilty for struggling with what is actually a devastating (health) problem. It will most likely confirm to the infertile person that there are very few people who really appreciate the depths they are suffering, and it will increase their sense of isolation. One friend recalls how someone once very tritely said to her, 'You don't *need* to have children.' Of course we don't 'need' children in the same way that we need food and shelter to survive. But my friend described how that comment summarily 'dismissed all my God-given emotions … which stem from my very physiology as a woman'. Others will glibly quote Scripture at a hurting infertile person. They may say, 'Just remember, God works all things for the good of those who love Him!' Again, it is kindly meant (and true, of course). But this is not usually helpful when given in such a manner. The infertile person may well switch off to any further 'help' at this point.

Some caring people may suggest reasons for infertility that seem very spiritual, such as, 'You can do more in the church, or go on the mission field.' This really may be true for some; Nick and I can actually see something of that in our own lives—but it will never be true for all infertile couples. And besides, many Christian couples with children of their own do all these things too: most of the missionary couples we know have their own children. Some people have tried to suggest retrospectively that God may have prevented a pregnancy because He knew that later on one of the couple would struggle with a serious illness, such as cancer. Perhaps one of them will die young. Others suggest that maybe it is 'for the best', as perhaps all our children would have been severely disabled and we 'might not have coped'. I do not find it helpful to try to guess at precise reasons as to why God has allowed this trial in our lives. It *may* be a mix of all the above and more, but also it may not. Some of His dealings with us will surely remain a mystery in this life. We know that His ways are entirely beyond and above ours. I believe sometimes we must just work at trusting in the Lord's providence, wisdom and goodness, rather than trying to find reasons for everything, especially in other people's lives.

I personally have been most receptive to suggestions that being childless can be positive from those who have walked this path themselves.

'Have you ever thought about adopting?'

I have one friend who, ever since her childhood, has longed to adopt vulnerable children. Upon discovering her own infertility, therefore, she did not mind being asked this question. However, this (and the many variations on it) is perhaps one question that many infertile couples find most difficult yet are consistently asked. The immediate answer which usually springs to my mind is, 'Yes! We are childless! *Of course* we have thought about adoption—and indeed about any other possible option available that could remedy our painful situation!' Immediately after asking this question, some enquirers will then continue to describe in detail just how marvellous a solution it has been for someone they know. This can actually make an already awkward situation even more unbearable for the infertile person. Of course, adoption *is* for some childless couples a truly wonderful way of building a family. Nick and I haven't ruled it out; we may yet consider it, and that is now my standard answer to the question. We have several friends who are simply fantastic examples of commitment and love to children who needed a loving home. And, on the other hand, surely adopting does not need to be the domain solely of the childless? We know an increasing number of wonderful couples who have adopted a child in addition to bearing their own children. They have done this simply because they longed to give a loving, stable home to a needy youngster. Indeed, sometimes when we have been asked 'Why don't you adopt?' Nick has confessed that he has almost asked back, 'Why don't you?'(!)

Most adoptive parents are overwhelmingly positive about adoption, and have found real fulfilment themselves in the family life it has brought them. Nevertheless, not every couple, not even the childless, consider it to be the way forward for them. Some couples are struggling so much with the bitter grief of being unable to have their own baby that they are not yet ready to consider adoption. At that stage of their bereavement, they may be struggling with a sense of total loss, which nothing else can actually replace. We know of some women who have discovered that, even after adopting *and* loving their adopted child/children very much, they are still aching to conceive and bear their own biological child. We have also known it to be the adoptive father who, while finding great happiness with his new family, continues to long for a biological child.

It is also important to consider that for some who do begin the adoption process, the procedure is not always completely straightforward these days. Young babies up for adoption in the UK are now generally in much shorter supply than in years past. Not everyone feels they could manage the adoption of an older child or, as is becoming more common now, a ready-made family of several children. Some couples (like us) may in their earlier, pre-infertile lives have been sure that if childless, they would 'definitely' adopt. But perhaps after years of unsuccessful medical intervention they feel so battered and bruised that they wonder if their emotional health would be able to withstand the two years of highly detailed preparation by adoption agencies. A couple's experience of the adoption process may vary considerably depending on where they live in the UK. Certain adoption authorities require prospective adopting couples to live near to their own extended family, as additional support.

Local authorities will also differ in their requirements and sympathy towards a couple's religious beliefs. Indeed, we know one couple who were rejected by an adoption panel because of their evangelical faith. I have also heard it said that couples have been turned down by agencies or local authorities for the following reasons: being too middle class, having too many books in the house, being too old, or being too financially poor. Sadly, in recent years, some of the UK agencies that might have been more sympathetic regarding faith issues (many Catholic ones, for example) have been compelled to close down. (Editorial note: An exciting new Christian adoption and fostering agency/charity has been established since this chapter was originally written. It is called Home for Good; website details are available in Appendix 1.)

All of this is not written to focus on the negatives; it is simply that we would not want anyone to bolster a couple up with unrealistic or even false hopes of building their family through adoption, as it may not work out for everyone. As with fertility treatments, couples need to be aware of the pitfalls, and have some time and space to make sense of their emotions before exploring this option. Indeed, a friend who has recently adopted two young boys emphasized that adoption agencies now want to be certain that a childless couple have arrived at some sense of peace with their infertility before embarking upon this course.

Not a few people have urged me, 'You should adopt … I know someone who did, and then she fell pregnant naturally!' Apart from the fact that this outcome apparently happens only in about 5 per cent of cases, I have never thought that adoption should be the means to that sort of end. How would the adopted child feel if they thought they were second-best? Most adoptive parents will want others to see this option as a very positive choice and a wonderful new direction in their lives, just as it is for their adopted child. It is simply not a last-ditch attempt at happiness; it is certainly not scraping the bottom of the barrel in the hope that something 'better' will eventually come along.

Above all, however, the casual suggestion of adoption being a quick and easy solution to the problem of childlessness seems to negate the very complex problems and emotions with which many infertile couples are struggling so much. Lois Flowers, who now has very happily adopted two children, describes her own response to the 'adoption' question. She explains that the lack of a baby is not the only issue in infertility:

> If I had to rank all the thoughtless things people say from most to least hurtful, the phrase 'You can always adopt' would be right up there at the top of the list. I know adoption sounds like a logical solution to the problem of childlessness. However, a glib comment like this fails to address all the painful questions and issues that not being able to conceive brings up in a person's life. As wonderful as it is, adoption does not

automatically erase all the physical brokenness, theological confusion and emotional distress that infertility causes.[1]

Fostering children in need of temporary loving care is, of course, another option for infertile couples, and one in which some will find fulfilment. In some cases, the children may then remain with them permanently. Fostering is not simply the domain of the childless, however, as many couples with their own children foster and, as mentioned previously, even adopt. We have some friends who were struggling to conceive over forty years ago now and their doctor advised them to foster. After this, they soon had their first baby on the way, and they believe it was the different focus that helped them to relax. They actually continued to foster long after their own four children were born. However, we know another long-term childless couple who found certain aspects of fostering very difficult, while dearly loving the children in their care. Those little ones were eventually moved on and, to be honest, I have often wondered at how doubly bereft some infertile couples might feel when they do eventually have to return a child with whom they have perhaps bonded closely and begun to love as if their own. For some of them, it might all be too deeply upsetting and unsettling; I wonder how I would face it myself, although we haven't ruled this out yet either.

So adoption (or fostering) can be, and often is, a very positive response to the situation of childlessness. It is surely a biblical response, given that God has actually 'adopted' us, Christians, to be His children. I am certainly not trying to put off any prospective adoptive or foster parents; we are very excited for and admire our friends who are considering it, and for those who are already building their families that way. Many if not most of them eventually say that to adopt was the best decision they have ever made. However, it is extremely unhelpful for acquaintances to exert what the childless couple may interpret as pressure, so that they have to give excuses for not proceeding with adoption, fostering, or even fertility treatments. These are personal and complicated issues, and most infertile couples we know do not like being put on the spot concerning them.

Likewise, it is so upsetting when a couple need to combat suggestions that they 'cannot really have wanted children all that much' because they have not adopted, fostered or undergone medical intervention. It is also unlikely that an infertile person will wish to start a discussion on all the benefits and drawbacks of these options at a party, conference or church lunch! As a rule, if an infertile couple want to discuss adoption, fostering or fertility treatments, they will probably seek out someone they trust to do this with, at a time when they are ready. Notwithstanding the fact that all of these 'solutions' have been a wonderful outcome and choice for many couples, others clearly believe that God is leading them along different paths.

Facing thoughtless assumptions

One friend who has lived with childlessness for many years recently remarked how, in the early days, her friends with babies assumed that she knew very little about children. She was rarely asked to babysit for them when they were small (perhaps it was assumed that she wouldn't want to). Yet this friend already had several years' teaching experience. Obviously, those of us who have no children of our own will have limits to our experience: some much more than others. Some of us definitely will not have much confidence in handling little ones, and admittedly there are going to be times when we get it wrong while trying to care for somebody else's children. Sometimes I do need to swallow my own feelings and *not* keep thinking, 'If I were the mother …' (After all, I am *not* the mother!) But it can be hurtful to childless women (or men) to assume they know nothing at all about children and family life. Indeed, many of the infertile women I know maintain positions as doctors, midwives, nurses, teachers, nannies, speech therapists or in other caring professions.

Other people can assume the childless chose their situation. Comments like, 'Well, you have always been a career woman, you never really wanted children anyway, did you?' can be hard to swallow. One friend struggled from constant assumptions like this in her church. The comments were made in ignorance, but she decided not to reveal the real reason why she did not have children. She said how she preferred the insensitivity to be unwitting, as she didn't think she could cope with nasty comments made knowingly. Even worse can be statements such as, 'I think it is really selfish when couples don't have/choose not to have children.' Is it? Perhaps in some cases it *might* be. But who are we to judge? Is it not also occasionally possible that some fertile people choose to *have* children for what we might consider to be 'selfish' reasons? I have known people who have chosen not to have children because their own childhoods were very unhappy and they doubt their ability to be good parents. Perhaps such couples are actually trying to be realistic and responsible. Others do not have their own children because of already diagnosed congenital complications. They might have loved the opportunity to be parents. We so often condemn others without knowing their full story.

Some people make public and vocal assumptions on how they plan to build their families: 'We'll wait for three years and then have our first baby.' Or, 'I'll get pregnant at Christmas … then we'll space them out every two years.' Perhaps many of us thought along these lines early on in our marriages. But infertile couples, those who have learned the hard way, can struggle when they are at the receiving end of such comments.

Sifting through well-meant but unsought advice

Many of us have been told, 'Just relax … that's all you need to do!' Or, 'You're trying too hard!' Or, 'You want a baby too much!' I do think it may make a difference if some of us who are worrying types learn ways to relax and ease tension. It will certainly make a difference to our quality of life. But actually, with some medical conditions (such as fallopian tube absence), relaxing will not make a jot of difference. And after some months of unsuccessful trying, even the most placid couple can become anxious. Just telling an infertile couple to relax and forget about it will probably not make that happen. In fact, telling them to 'just forget about it' is usually asking them to do the impossible, especially if they are undergoing medical intervention. For almost two years of our infertility programme, Nick and I were daily charting and timing my monthly cycle. At other times I was also taking medication, some of which was injected daily, and having blood tests every week. Of course we thought about it all the time: we couldn't forget it! Could anyone else have done otherwise? Likewise, it is impossible to just stop wanting a baby, as if our emotions and biological longings can be switched off on command. And as described before, those who are suffering greatly over their situation will be plunged afresh into new grief every month. We cannot 'just forget'. It takes time to arrive at a situation of peace. I believe that the Lord can bring true and lasting peace, but much prayer is needed, and practical help, rather than admonition, is always appreciated.

Sometimes people will overwhelm their infertile friends with stories about 'little miracles' or amazing treatments that worked for another couple. We do appreciate sensitive and kind efforts to keep us encouraged, and once again, we try to rejoice with those who rejoice. As described previously, we may well consider trying the new course of action for ourselves. Nick and I have often tried out suggestions given to us. They have sometimes been very useful in boosting our general health and mental attitude. But please also remember that, in terms of becoming pregnant, it just may not work for us, or for another childless couple, and we might not want to be disappointed yet again.

It can also be very hard for a couple to be told unequivocally (usually by a fertile Christian), 'Oh no! You can't do [name of treatment].' Or the opposite: 'You are just not trying enough! You should try […].' I personally know the feeling of wanting to try anything at all, even though we have not actually done so. However, as stated above in our own story, there were certain options we would not pursue having researched into them ourselves and discussed them with our minister and others. We have also turned down other treatments simply because we did not think it helpful to our already fragile emotions to continue. Nick and I try not to condemn point-blank any infertile couple following a certain course of treatment, even if we believe it to be unethical. We might gently present any relevant alternative options in the light of biblical ethics. We as Christians are called to help and question each other if there are grave concerns, and to remind one another of what God has revealed in his Word. But Nick and I do this knowing first-hand the desperation of being unhappily childless. We try to follow Jesus' example of combining biblical teaching with his tender compassion and mercy for those who are suffering what may well be the greatest grief of their lives.

Among close friends and family, we are usually happy to discuss our feelings or possibilities about treatment. But again, not all infertile people will be: it really is a matter of getting to know the people concerned. Indeed, some childless couples we know have sadly experienced a lack of sympathy from their own families on these issues. Others are thrown into confusion and guilt by family or friendship pressures to follow a course of action which goes against their conscience. Please do not let that happen to any loved ones you know who are infertile.

Mothering Sunday or Father's Day gaffes

Mothering Sunday or Father's Day can be especially painful if the childless are entirely overlooked. I desperately struggled through one service when a visiting preacher prayed in some detail for all mothers and the unique work they do. He handed out presents for all the mothers, and then for all the men (not just fathers) so that they didn't feel left out. But as I didn't fall into either category I was the only adult in that small gathering who was given nothing. I do not know how I got through that service. I felt the sympathy of all around, and not wanting to be ostentatious by walking out, sat there with my tears silently flowing until I could make my escape during the last hymn. I remember nothing else of that service. The minister was not from the UK and it was Mothering Sunday in his country, but not in ours. Nick was away, and sadly it also happened to be the day I realized our fertility programme had failed for the final time. I know that the preacher's intentions had been good as he was very sorry about it afterwards. It was not so much the lack of a present from the front that hurt (although that did hurt), but mainly the fact that I felt of no consequence at all, because I was not a mother and yet so desperately wanted to be one.

I know another childless pastor's wife who received no flowers in church one Mothering Sunday, as all the women were supposed to, because she was sat alone at the front. Her husband who was leading the service could not see what was happening, and it seemed that nobody else did either. The greatest of care needs to be taken in such church services that we have no brothers or sisters who are left feeling needlessly out in the cold. Otherwise, do not be surprised if some never come back, at least on Mother's or Father's Day. 'Family Services' containing a huge emphasis on the nuclear family can be equally difficult for singles and childless couples. Unless care is taken to include them as well they may be left feeling like mere observers at the service, rather than worshippers of God.

'I'm pregnant ... again!'

Many struggling childless couples' own grief has been compounded by insensitive pregnancy announcements. Perhaps a struggling and emotional woman has just made it through a church service. Perhaps she is infertile or has recently lost a baby. Her emotions are raw and sensitive. She is about to leave the busy group quietly, but is stopped on her way by a bouncing and highly excited fellow church member who bursts out, 'Guess what! I'm pregnant!'—and who then continues to discuss how wonderful it is, right there and then. This actually happened to a good friend of mine. It is a common problem childless or bereaved couples face in their own church, and throughout the wider church network, but also in friendship and family situations.

Some ministers announce such news from the pulpit at the start of a service. It can be desperately difficult to be suddenly faced with that unexpected news in public, or in front of the couple themselves, and to have to respond somehow. Everyone else is buzzing, but the grieving couple will probably just want to run away, sob, or even scream about how unfair it all is. At that point, they may not even be able to force a smile.

I have found that, when struggling, it really helps to know the news of new pregnancies in advance. Then I can deal with my initial reactions in private. As one friend so aptly puts it, 'I can set my face straight' for when she next attends church, work, or meets the expectant couple. Hopefully by then, through God's help, she may be able to smile and give a genuine congratulation. It can be a surprise, even sometimes a shock, to hear of a new pregnancy. Thoughtful messages warning us in advance will also be appreciated when the new baby is born, or has a christening, thanksgiving or dedication service.

Discussions about other people's children

Sometimes an infertile woman may unwillingly become party to conversations among fertile people on subjects such as how many (more) children they want, and what gender or physical and mental characteristics they desire in their offspring. Some may even complain about those whom they have already been given! This may, of course, be in jest, but it still does not help. To an unhappily childless person who just longs for the gift of a baby, such talk can make children seem little more than accessories, and it can lead to struggles with resentment of the fertile couples who just do not seem to appreciate how much they have been blessed. I have also found it difficult to sit in on conversations with fertile women who are discussing various aspects of gynaecology, or to hear others' opinions as to what age a woman should give up the idea of having children.

It may also seem obvious that it is unhelpful for a happily fertile couple to talk much in the presence of an infertile person about how quick, easy, unexpected or wonderful it was for them to have children, or to make jokes about how it happened for them. But interestingly, the opposite does not usually help either. Of course, no childless woman would usually begrudge a struggling pregnant woman some sympathy and help. I have known a number of women who have been hospitalized by pregnancy, some even seeming near death, and who had a truly unenviable nine months or a terribly traumatic birth. I am not talking about that. But when a happily pregnant woman complains about all the discomfort and disadvantages of having a baby (being sick, tired, 'fat', hot, uncomfortable, and so on) in order to 'help' a childless woman present, it does not usually cause that childless woman to be glad that she is not pregnant. I am sure it has usually been kindly meant, to try to help us realize that it is not all plain sailing. But most infertile women have observed something of the trials of pregnancy anyway, and would still more than willingly go through such just to have a baby of their own. They may wonder if some people really do appreciate the amazing gift they have been given. It can be so tempting to snap, 'Well, at least you are pregnant—you should be grateful! It is only for nine months … and what I wouldn't give to be in your shoes.' As detailed before, some childless couples will have already struggled with enormous medical trauma anyway in their attempts to conceive. Some will be living with chronic physical symptoms connected with the reason behind their infertility; for example, endometriosis is often excruciatingly painful. Most infertile couples are sure that in many cases, after a baby is born, the trials of the actual pregnancy are forgotten in the joy of a new life: most of these women will, after all, be wanting (and soon having) more babies! Furthermore, we know too that most of these parents adore their children and wouldn't be without them for the world.

I clearly remember a time, long ago now, when the childless daughter of a friend finally became pregnant after years of infertility heartache and one very early miscarriage. I asked if her daughter was feeling sick. The answer was something like, 'Yes, badly, and from about three weeks. And she is *delighted* to be sick!' My friend would not hear otherwise. Being sick meant her daughter was pregnant, *and continuing to be pregnant*. Now she finally had real hope of a baby to be born.

Chapter 6

'I have great hope for you!'

Since our miscarriage, a few very kind and caring people have asked us, 'Are you still trying?' Or even, 'Is God still withholding?' I know that there is an element of hope there, and that for some the question is asked in order to inform their prayers. But apart from thinking how awkward it would be if I actually *was* in the early stages of pregnancy and didn't want to mention it at that time, I actually feel under pressure when asked this sort of question. I usually murmur something vague about how 'trying hurts', or, 'Well, of course, we would still very much love to have a baby …' but admitting to be 'still trying' rams home rather painfully to me our continued failure in this area.

Considering the subject of hope, one phrase that very kind and caring people have urged me with over the years is, 'Don't give up hope' or, 'I have great hope for you.' It is a kindness that needs to be used carefully. Now I know that we need to keep up our hope in God's goodness, and in His *ability* to give us children. But as I have already described, to nurture hope of an actual pregnancy each month, or to have our hopes entirely set on a human 'cure', but never see it fulfilled, can deepen the heartbreak and depression. Some people, surely in an effort to keep our spirits up, have said, 'I just *know* you will have a baby one day!' Or, 'It'll be your turn next!' Apart from wondering how they can know that when I do not, such predictions can also be pressurizing. What if I fail to live up to these expectations? Will I have to live with their disappointment too?

Some people will make their gut feelings or hopes sound more spiritual: 'God told me you were going to have a baby', or, 'I had a dream from the Lord that you had a baby, and it is going to happen soon!' The fact is, people can be wrong, and it might be best to keep these thoughts, words or dreams to themselves, until after the baby has indeed been conceived and born. As I emphasized before, the constant disappointment is one of the hardest aspects of infertility to bear. You do not want to make it even harder. I was recently struck by the Shunammite woman's story in 2 Kings 4. This woman had 'no son', and her husband was 'old' (v. 14). When Elisha promised her a son for the next year, this was her plaintive response: 'No, my lord … Don't mislead your servant, O man of God!' (v. 16). Of course, in this case God really had spoken through Elisha, His prophet. But long-term infertile women can relate to that cry—to the desire *not* to have hopes raised only to be dashed again, after too many years of disappointment.

The friend mentioned previously who knew years of supporting her then childless daughter remarked to me how hope will pop up, month after month. As mentioned earlier, we may start thinking, 'Wow, I am feeling a bit sick … maybe this time …' But my friend urged me, 'You need to squash that hope!' At first, that seemed harsh, and certainly almost impossible to do. But now, years later, I can see what she meant. She did not mean for me to become morbid: to give up on life, or on God's sovereignty or goodness in the situation. But she meant for me to develop realism, and to focus consciously and purposefully on other ways of serving God. I accepted this from her because she knew what she was talking about, and my emotional health has been strongest when I have been able to do that.

Some practical ideas for helping an infertile couple are listed at the end of Chapter 7.

Chapter 6

Pause for thought

- Take time to write out two or three sentences you can use in response when people ask you about your situation.
- Practise saying these sentences so that your pace of speech and tone of voice convey what you intend.
- Pray about those situations when you have been hurt by others.

Bible passages for reflection

For the LORD gives wisdom,
and from his mouth come knowledge and understanding.
(Prov. 2:6)

A fool shows his annoyance at once,
but a prudent man overlooks an insult.
Reckless words pierce like a sword,
but the tongue of the wise brings healing. (Prov. 12:16, 18)

A word aptly spoken
is like apples of gold in settings of silver. (Prov. 25:11)

When they hurled their insults at him [Jesus], he did not retaliate; when he suffered, he made no threats. Instead, he entrusted himself to him who judges justly. (1 Peter 2:23)

Prayers

A) FOR THE CHILDLESS

Almighty God, you are the Judge of all. You will judge rightly, because you are perfectly just, and nothing is hidden from you. You see behind our words and deeds to the thoughts within. Thank you for the peace that gives me, as I leave judgement to you. I confess that I scarcely know my own mind at times, and cannot truly know the minds of others. But you know how I have found certain comments and questions about my situation so hard to deal with. You know how I have felt pierced to the heart by insensitive remarks, or worn down by repeated questioning. Give me a thick skin to bear insensitive and even callous words. But you know too when the person was just trying to be helpful and offer comfort or advice, and you don't show favouritism among your children. Help them to be thoughtful and sensitive; give them understanding, so that they can successfully bring the help that they intend. But please sanctify my attitudes and responses. Forgive me when I have spoken inappropriately or harboured bitterness within. Help me to hold my tongue when I feel provoked. Help me to think the best of them. Help me to love them. Through the power of your name, Amen.

B) FOR THE HELPER

Merciful Father, you love every one of your children with a passion. When we sin against each other you are grieved. When we cause each other pain by the things we do or say, or by withholding what we can give, we offend you. As I consider my fellow brothers and sisters in Christ who struggle with infertility, I'm aware that I've not been the loving Christian that I should have been, perhaps through ignorance of what was needed, or perhaps through thoughtlessness. In your mercy, forgive me for those times I have brought further grief to these children of yours. Forgive me for when my words and actions have been uncaring or insensitive. Forgive me when I have been negligent in loving them. Teach me how I can bring your love effectively. Your Word is a lamp to our feet; help me to learn how to shine it sensitively and appropriately, so that I don't blind them when their eyes are delicate. In Jesus' name, Amen.

Part 3 Help for the childless

Part 3

So after all this ... has there been *any* comfort in our trial of infertility? And equally important: How do we stop our pain in the situation developing into sinfully established behavioural patterns? How do we prevent our devastation becoming hardened bitterness, our disappointment becoming ungodly disillusionment, our sense of comparison becoming destructive jealousy, and our depression becoming self-pity? How do we prevent our desperation becoming recklessness? How do we stop our natural longing for a family becoming an obsession or an idol? How do we give our situation into the Lord's hands, and learn to leave it with Him?

Perhaps in some, even many, situations counselling or other medical support may be necessary to help a distressed couple regain some mental composure. But alongside this, Nick and I have increasingly discovered that our greatest source of strength and help has been through knowing our gracious God in increasing depth: through His Word, and through the love of His people.

Recently I have grown to love a poignant and beautiful song entitled 'In the Valley' (further details can be found in Appendix 1). It is based on an old Puritan prayer. One verse begins thus:

> In the daytime there are stars in the heavens
> But they only shine at night
> And the deeper that I go into darkness
> The more I see their radiant light.[1]

It is a precious realization that often we begin truly to experience the hitherto veiled qualities and beauty of God when we are in the darkness of pain. Surely our faith and trust are truly tested only during difficult trials. It is then that we are shown up for what we are, and God is shown for who He really is. It is then that God demonstrates to us the great 'stars' of all His magnificent attributes and glory. He bestows His power to help us in our weaknesses and develops in us 'stars' of Christian character: He transforms us to be increasingly more like Jesus.

So, mercifully, there is indeed help to be found in our trials. Even throughout our darkest times, and in countless ways, God has been very good to Nick and myself, and to our other infertile friends. Sometimes I have not been able to see the goodness of God when I have been really struggling in a pit of depression. There have been, and occasionally still are, some days when nothing much seems to help. But I am profoundly thankful to God for even the smallest means by which His compassionate love to us has been shown. I am able to see His hand throughout all our years of struggle, right up to this day.

I have been longing to reach this section of the book, though I must warn you that it is not a 'quick-fix' formula to overcoming infertility grief. I am certainly not 'there' yet myself. However, despite it being a very rocky road with many setbacks, with God there is life beyond infertility, and we can grow through the distress. It may be many years before we are finally able to let go of our dreams of a (biological) baby of our own and be at peace with God's providence, fully trusting that all He does is good and for our best. However, we pray that, no matter how long it takes for God to do this work in us, our resulting 'stars' of Christlike lives will glow ever brighter, illuminating the lives of others in this dark and hurting world.

Chapter 7

Experiencing love and care from others

In the bleakest times of our experience, the care of others has been a lifeline. It is as though God Himself has been there in the arms, ears and voices of those who love us, to help us bear this burden. At times I have not been able to sense Him any other way. Of course, we have the continued support of each other. We are blessed also to have caring families. Our parents in particular have always been there for us and have helped us in every way possible. We appreciate their love and concern more than we can express. But in addition to that there have been many others, close friends from many years back and among the church families where we have belonged over the years. I do believe they are a great example to follow. Nick and I have also been blessed with very positive church experiences throughout our trial of infertility. Disappointingly, this will not be so for every infertile couple. We hope, in part, that our story here will be an encouragement and helpful example to churches who have an unhappily childless couple living in their midst. One of the most important aspects of support has been from those who have helped me to grieve effectively. Those who have supported me best have acknowledged and sympathized with the reality and depths of our loss, not dismissing or undermining my feelings. They have not been shocked by my strong emotions, and have not expected too much from me when I have been unable to give anything back. They have also, with gentleness and appropriateness, nudged us to the place where we can find the best of help: back to God and His Word.

After our initial shocking diagnosis in 2001, our then pastor's wife suggested that she and the other elders' wives tell every woman in the church that Nick and I were struggling to conceive. There was another couple also struggling with infertility, so they would be included too. At first I was reluctant; after all, it was such a personal issue. However, we were assured that no particular medical details would be broadcast and no questions asked; it was primarily so the church family could pray for us. We agreed. For me at least, it was the best suggestion our pastor's wife could have made.

The resulting outpouring of care and kindness from many in the church at that time was an indescribable comfort. They listened, prayed, gently and appropriately reminded me of spiritual truth, gave small gifts, tactfully lent helpful books and any other resources they could find, and took me for days out. They held me as I cried, and expressed their own sadness at our situation. They encouraged me to pour out my heartbreak, disappointment, confusion and even anger to God, who knew exactly how I felt anyway. 'He can take it!' one friend assured me. Most of the insensitive comments, which had been made in ignorance prior to the situation being made known, ceased. Those who knew me a bit better checked up on me regularly to see how I was doing, and continued to do so later, as our treatment progressed. One elder's wife phoned me every time she knew there was a new pregnancy about to be announced in church, just so that I was prepared. The women who were having new babies treated us with sensitivity. One good friend even told me tactfully and discreetly that she and her husband were going to start trying for a baby! She was so sensitive in trying to prepare me for any possible news that would come. She then phoned me a short time later when they had good news. I was staggered by her thoughtfulness. She explained that she and her husband felt privileged to have been given a child, and that it was something they did not take for granted. Not having experienced infertility herself, she later asked me how best she could support me: what was helpful for her to say and do, or not helpful. Again, I was amazed by her honesty and her willingness to admit being rather out of her depth.

This experience of having such a private issue opened up, even in a supportive church setting, may not be something every infertile couple feel they could endure. We are all very different. For us, the experience was humbling in that we essentially admitted in public to having a major and irresolvable problem, albeit one not of our own making. But more importantly, it helped us realize that we do not need to carry burdens alone, and that there are many people who will do all they can to help someone who is hurting. If we had not opened up, we would not have known such love. It helped me to become a little more open with people generally, about this and about other issues in life, which perhaps, on balance, can be helpful in a church setting. I am sure any struggling couple will benefit from sharing their trial and burden with at least a few others whom they can trust.

As we have moved around the country and attended other churches, God has provided us with equally caring support. We had one pastor who taught the congregation about the issue of infertility using passages such as Luke 1, which emphasizes the godliness of the childless Zechariah and Elizabeth. This attempted to dispel the notion that infertility is necessarily anything to do with a couple's sinfulness. After the especially distressing Mothering Sunday experience described earlier, I was again aware of God's love through His people. Several stood comforting me for over an hour outside the building afterwards, while I sobbed. One dear lady gave me her own 'Mother's Present', a very kind couple cared for me in their home for the entire day, and another lady brought flowers to our home the following morning. This level of care seemed to me to be outstanding.

During the time of our miscarriage (and still continuing now) we have been aware of the earnest prayers and loving concern of our Mirfield congregation. When the trauma hit, people brought us meals, sent flowers and beautiful cards, and helped us with domestic tasks. They sat and talked with me when I was in blackness. They prayed earnestly. We feel that God used this to bond us more deeply with our church family.

The kindness of God has also been shown to us from our extended family and friends who live far away. Some have helped with the cost of private treatments, or provided time away for us when we have been especially sad. We know of many who pray for us regularly, sometimes over the phone, and others have written encouraging letters, or sent us beautiful hymns and poems. As I write this, Nick and I have just finally sealed away all the cards sent to us after our miscarriage. We were struck by the love that they contain, for the compassion and attempts to walk with us in our pain. Some thoughtful friends even sent messages and flowers at the time our baby would have been due, which meant more to us than I can tell. People really have tried to understand what we are going through.

Some friends have patiently listened for hours on the telephone while I have cried, attempting to unravel my feelings about the whole situation. One dear friend discovered she was (very happily) pregnant for the first time, when we had already been trying a number of years. She sobbed down the phone, 'I just wish it were you, rather than me …' I was humbled by her selflessness, and wondered if I could ever have had the big-heartedness to feel like that for somebody else.

We have been grateful for the assurance that our family and friends love and highly value us just as we are, that they do not consider us disappointments or failures because we have not produced any children. We are thankful when they include us in their family life, when we are feeling strong enough. I was grateful then, and still am, for those women who will let me hold their babies and talk to me about them, but who do not assume that because I could cope on that one day, I would be completely fine from then on. Of course there are times when maybe for a long while we are fine, and then we just appreciate being treated normally!

Considering all the above, Nick and I suggest that it is vital for a suffering infertile Christian couple to be wholly involved in the life of a helpful and caring church. A couple's own family of origin may be far away (our families are), but as Christians we are part of God's family. This spiritual family, expressed in the local church, is of all ages, abilities, social classes, and should know no divisions due to whether or not we are married or have children. This family will last us into eternity.

There may well be times when it feels just too difficult to attend a particular meeting. As mentioned before, church services can bring strong emotions to the fore, and simply sitting behind a young baby or happy family may be too much on some days. But to stay away indefinitely, or slowly drop off the radar altogether, will surely never help in the end. As Christians living in the world we need each other so much. In church, we should all be able to receive (and give) love, care and nurture. We will benefit from meeting together as a body to worship God even if on some days the hymns do make us crumple. We need the encouragement, the challenge, the comfort and sometimes the rebuke of sitting under a regular preaching ministry each week. We need to find help and accountability, not just in our infertility, but in all other aspects of our Christian walk. Infertile couples have just as much to offer the body of Christ as couples who have children, though sometimes in different ways. We all have our particular gifts, talents and experiences with which to help others and contribute to the richness of church life. It is vital that a local church family makes efforts to include and affirm those who feel isolated due to infertility, and that the couple themselves make their best efforts to be involved.

The fact that Nick and I have been enabled to cope so far with our situation is, as we emphasized initially, entirely through God's grace. Part of this is that we have both been blessed over many years, even since before we met each other, to sit under faithful Bible teaching in church, and for myself also, as a child, in a regular youth Bible class. We therefore already had a framework in place for when the tough times hit hard. Having previously been taught about suffering, and God's sovereignty and purposes in it, has given us a backbone of solid support in those dark times when we cannot *feel* God's love. Perhaps one of the other ways in which God has best used other Christians throughout our trial is through them (tactfully) applying biblical principles to our situation. This has often been during informal times together. It has helped to be gently 'drip-fed' spiritual truth over the years.

A good friend of ours recently led a seminar on infertility at her church ladies' meeting. She asked me for a few suggestions on how concerned church members could help those whose struggles with the problem are public knowledge. If you are someone who wishes to help an infertile friend(s), please do remember that those in the early stages of infertility, or after a major setback, may feel they are in a state of perpetual bereavement. Please treat them as you would any other grieving person: with utmost sensitivity. Remember that they may erupt in tears at any moment, perhaps even in the years to come. So here, in conclusion to this chapter, is a summary of what has been helpful for us, and may therefore be helpful for an infertile couple you know:

- Listen to them, allowing them to acknowledge, describe and vent their feelings and explore the emotions evoked by their infertility. This may be repeated time and again, as they attempt to weather the storm.
- If you simply do not know how to respond, perhaps it is best to say very little, other than to assure them that you are so very sorry, and that, even if you cannot understand the depths of their suffering,

they have your love, concern and prayers. You could ask them what would be the best way for you to help them.

- Think very carefully before saying anything much more than the above—particularly before offering platitudes, rebukes, advice, your own thoughts about their position or comparisons of their situation with anyone else's (favourably or otherwise). Each person's experience of pain is very individual, and of course none of us has ever stepped exactly into another's shoes.
- Try to avoid pressurizing them into, or out of, any particular course of action. That is for them to decide, under God. If you believe that they are acting unwisely or even sinfully, bring it to the Lord yourself and ask Him for wisdom on how to approach the subject with them.
- Let them know beforehand, and in private, when a new pregnancy is to be announced in church, the wider community, or even within their family situation, allowing them to 'set their face straight' before facing other people's response to the news. I have always found sensitive texts, emails and, in particular, kind letters from the expectant mother to be the most helpful here. But it is also helpful if another person (not one of the couple themselves) phones me.
- Be sensitive in how you talk about your own or other people's pregnancies, children, grandchildren and family life in front of them.
- Remember that a church with many babies and seemingly happy families may be one of the places they will struggle most, so give them space when they are finding it hard. On the other hand, if they have missed church for a while, make sure you keep up with them, and encourage them to return, both for their own spiritual benefit and for that of the whole church. The entire church family misses out while they are absent.
- Some childless couples really appreciate being able to be involved in the lives of other people's children and like opportunities to be regularly (or occasionally) included in their family life. Others do not. Ask them if you are not sure!
- Please try not to just quickly quote well-known Scriptures at them. This very rarely helps anyone, as it can seem so insensitive, and sometimes the verses are taken out of context anyway. Those

who know the Bible well will know the verses already! An infertile couple obviously do need to know God's Word and apply it to their situation, but in a sensitive and prayerful context, with those they trust.

- One very helpful way we have received spiritual encouragement in our infertility trial is by caring friends giving us details of relevant books, websites and CDs which confirm biblical truth (some of these are listed in Appendix 1).
- You do not need to think that you have to provide all the 'right' spiritual answers all the time. Just continue to assure them that, above all, you are there for them and are willing to talk.
- It helps to be taken out for coffee or other relaxing activities, just so we can forget our problems for a while and talk about other, 'normal' things in life (I know one woman who was bought a series of piano lessons by a friend as she waited for a baby). We do not *always* want to be crying and talking about our infertility ...
- The childless woman will probably appreciate an invitation to events such as baby showers: it is not nice to be deliberately excluded if she may be feeling strong enough (and actually able) to go. But it helps her to know that it is also completely fine if she chooses not to attend.
- And a note for the men of the church: please remember that the husband will be suffering too, though perhaps not so visibly. Please don't allow him to be neglected. Sadly, this can often happen. Make every effort to find ways of helpfully supporting him too—perhaps in some of the ways suggested above.

It is often mentioned that we need to 'earn the right' to say certain things to people. Also, it is often *how* things are said, and *why*, and by whom, more than the words themselves, which has the greatest bearing on how they impact a person. This advice is certainly true in helping someone with infertility. There is immense value in simply being loving, loyal and available, wherever possible, to the infertile person. If then there are times when you believe that a careful, sensitive rebuke is needed, your friend knows they can trust you in this too.

Pause for thought

- How much of your situation have you shared with trusted Christian friends?
- If you haven't shared your situation, think about doing so.
- Keep a diary of the ways God is directing his love and support to you through this experience.

Bible passages for reflection

Let us consider how we may spur one another on towards love and good deeds. Let us not give up meeting together, as some are in the habit of doing, but let us encourage one another—and all the more as you see the Day approaching. (Heb. 10:24–25)

Carry each other's burdens, and in this way you will fulfil the law of Christ. (Gal. 6:2)

Prayers

A) FOR THE CHILDLESS

O Lord, you are the compassionate and gracious God, slow to anger and abounding in steadfast covenant love and faithfulness. All your ways to your children are full of grace and love. You use your children as channels of peace and compassion, agents to bring grace to help in time of need. We find that your grace streams to us through one another. In your wisdom, you establish the local church to be the primary source of care. Thank you for the fellowship in which you have placed me.

Thank you so much for the blessing of having loving brothers and sisters in Christ. Thank you for all the words and gestures we receive of love and care, and for the encouragement it is to know of others quietly supporting us in prayer. You know how deeply others feel for me. But you also know how at times I struggle with church. Give me grace not to resist or spurn their efforts to show me your compassion. Help me not to be afraid to be honest and open with those who love me. Help me not to cut myself off from the healing ministry of your Word. Help me not to withdraw or hold back from the very means you give to bless me.

In your mercy, Amen.

B) FOR THE HELPER

Heavenly Father, you have profound compassion for those who suffer. You know just what they require in the depths of their distress. You appoint us to bring your help to those in need. I pray for those I know and love who are suffering with infertility. Use me to help them. I cannot know exactly what they are going through, and I fear saying or doing things that will be unhelpful and will cause even further pain. You know what they need to hear and receive, what will be most appropriate and beneficial. Guide me as I speak to them and seek to help them bear their burden. Give me apt words, wisdom to know when to be silent, and a practical response that will truly communicate your love and be the ministry they need. In the name of our loving Saviour, Amen.

Navigating the medical minefield

Knowing our options in detail

We have been greatly supported in thinking through the medical issues. As mentioned previously, increasing numbers of people are beginning publicly to question the ethics and procedures of certain assisted reproduction techniques. This includes various religious groups, but also others who claim no religious faith at all. Some who hold to more humanistic viewpoints have expressed concern about the individual embryo's right to life.

I was blessed when working for the (secular) charity LIFE, as there was a wealth of freely available literature in their office concerning the ethical, physical and emotional implications of various fertility treatments. LIFE's research is extremely thorough, and is very detailed about various aspects of several assisted conception techniques which we had not known before. I was in constant contact with very knowledgeable and caring colleagues who were always willing to talk and they helped us clarify our thinking on many issues. Nick and I think it is vital that any infertile Christian couple considering serious medical intervention be well grounded in medical and biblical ethics. They need to consider carefully all that Scripture says about unborn life, family life, disability, care for the weak, and the human body. Our pastors, sympathetic yet realistic doctors, friends and family were of much help in this area, and we are grateful to them all. There are several Christian publications and websites which have been invaluable to us; they are listed in Appendix 1. The books by John Ling have been particularly helpful to me.

As mentioned previously, many people with strong pro-life convictions may well prefer to steer clear of IVF. It is true that a few have reported that they have undergone this treatment in a manner which respected some of their concerns in this area. In 2010 an interesting article was published in *The Briefing* by Susan and Tim Ravenhall, who underwent a more 'natural' form of IVF.[1] They eventually conceived and carried a baby to full term. However, the article is particularly helpful in highlighting the enormous struggles the couple underwent to have their 'difficult' questions considered and answered by their medical team. Any couple considering medical intervention for infertility need to understand exactly what each proposed treatment would involve, including any possible negative emotional or physical outcomes. They need to be able to think carefully and without pressure through the many 'What if?'s and ask as many questions as possible directly to the doctors who propose the treatment. They need to scrutinize the small print before signing any forms. Couples may also need to consider the financial cost, as some have eventually drained all their savings on fertility treatments. Each couple needs to consider if the treatment is going to be the best use of their resources.

Nick and I carefully considered several available treatment options, developing clear thinking about what we would and would not do if we proceeded with any of them. Infertile couples must not allow themselves to be intimidated into doing something they are unhappy about or unsure of. They need to know their rights, as Christians know what they believe the Lord would have them do in the light of His Word, and stand their ground. They need to have an idea of how many times they would consider repeating a treatment (if appropriate) should it not work the first time. Perhaps if they are in doubt about a certain course of action, it may be wise to wait, research and pray some more before proceeding.

Happily, of course, as mentioned before, for many couples the treatment option they follow *will* result in the longed-for pregnancy and baby. Not a few known to us have attempted a programme, but conceived naturally just after it failed and they had given up!

It is perhaps worth mentioning that although many people know about our infertility, we have never advertised to all and sundry our thoughts about treatments. Neither did everybody know exactly what we were doing or when, as it would have put us under more pressure. We did not want to keep detailing the minutiae of where we were at in the proceedings. I think this was helpful as it gave us some protection and privacy. We do not always need to be explaining everything to others.

It is also worth adding that, although we have endured some very difficult consultations with certain specialist fertility doctors, we are grateful that all our GPs over the years have been very patient and helpful. We have also had the more recent privilege of speaking with a very caring and helpful Christian specialist in infertility and miscarriage, and the LIFE FertilityCare Programme (LFP) shone out as a beacon of hope.

We would encourage any couple to consider the LFP. The love and care we received from them was first-rate. It is a private treatment programme but is cost-effective. There are no ethical or moral dilemmas to consider. It is based on extensive research and uses NaPro Technology, a restorative treatment which also helps to identify and address reasons for infertility and miscarriage. It is 'body friendly', cooperating with the woman's natural cycle, and is less invasive than some other forms of fertility treatment. It is administered with the medical and emotional needs of each client carefully considered, so we were treated with dignity, as a unique couple. Every step was thoroughly explained, so we felt in control throughout the process, from beginning to end. The doctor and nurses worked extremely hard, sometimes well out of ordinary working hours, to ensure that all our needs were provided for. They were available at the end of the phone, and even helped us years later, during our pregnancy and miscarriage. Although in God's providence the programme did not work for us, as emphasized before, we are so glad for that year spent with the LFP. Interestingly, many other infertile couples have been blessed with children through using the LFP where all previous medical attempts for them (including several cycles of standard IVF) have failed. Indeed, Life FertilityCare live births are comparable with more invasive treatments anyway. And one further interesting outcome of our involvement with that particular fertility programme was that later we were sometimes sharing information with other medical staff which was new to them!

Accepting what cannot be changed

When I feel that my body has failed me, it is helpful to remember that the Bible teaches that our bodies are a gift from God, part of being made in His image, and for Christians, they are temples of the Holy Spirit. We therefore need to honour God in how we treat them. They generally work well otherwise and we have that to be thankful for. While we may not attempt to apply everything that we read in the self-help books, we do thank God for the vast resources we have available in the UK to keep ourselves healthy. Even if our efforts at eating a better diet, reducing stress, getting better-quality sleep and developing a more positive attitude do not result in a baby, hopefully our minds and bodies will be in a better condition to live life in general and to serve the Lord.

I find it comforting to remember that God, who designed every complex and intimate aspect of the universe, has perfectly known since conception the workings of every amazing cell in our bodies, certainly far better than any human being does. Reading through Psalm 139 again reassures us of this—I have included verses 1–16 at the end of Appendix 2. We believe that God does not make mistakes. I try to remember that, while any medical condition affecting my fertility is very distressing, and although I may therefore try to remedy the situation medically, if nothing changes or 'works' as a result of that intervention it is part of God's perfect will for the time being. Several caring women have wisely urged me to think positively about my body. It may not be functioning in all the ways I desire, especially reproductively, at the moment. But it is the body God gave me, and therefore what He planned for me currently to live with. As such it should perhaps be seen as an ally, not an enemy. And we also remember that our all-powerful God is capable of overcoming medical problems anyway, should that be part of His plan.

All the help given to us meant we were able to make decisions with which we were both comfortable, for which our consciences did not condemn us and which we do not regret. We trust and pray that God has been honoured through it all.

Pause for thought

- How are you responding to the medical and spiritual advice you are receiving?
- What effect is this advice having on your relationship with each other?
- What effect is this advice having on your relationship with God?

Bible passages for reflection

> If any of you lacks wisdom, he should ask God, who gives generously to all without finding fault, and it will be given to him. (James 1:5)
>
> Do not be anxious about anything, but in everything, by prayer and petition, with thanksgiving, present your requests to God. And the peace of God, which transcends all understanding, will guard your hearts and your minds in Christ Jesus. (Phil. 4:6–7)

Prayer

Almighty God, by your wisdom you created the heavens and the earth. You made me, and you know intimately how my body functions. You know the medical problems that we face as a couple: things we may not fully understand. Thank you that you heal many infertile couples today through wholesome medical intervention. Father, you are aware of my deep desire to have children, and of how that has been my great prayer. But we understand that we must honour you first. So, all-wise God, please give us wisdom as we consider medical assistance. Help us to discern what courses of action would be displeasing to you, and grant us the resolution to avoid them. Through Jesus, who has been tempted in every way like us, you know the temptation to try anything available, out of desperation. So please help us to hold fast to your principles, and give us strength if that should prove very painful. Give us the grace of Jesus to say, 'Yet not my will, but yours be done.' Amen.

Chapter 9

Safeguarding marriage

This chapter is short but vital. Nick and I have found it necessary to keep a careful watch over all the different aspects of our married life, to try to ensure that this trauma of infertility and miscarriage does not tear us apart. Nick has already admitted that he often shelved his own grief-stricken emotions in order to be my 'rock' during the hardest times. But he would now re-emphasize that God is the Rock for us both, and perhaps, had we cried to him together more often, that might have been more helpful.

Despite the above, it is also true that we have always tried to keep communication constant, honest and open between us, especially on what, if anything, to do about our childlessness. Such detailed discussions can take much patience, careful, respectful listening, and time. We have sometimes discovered it to be easier when away from home, when we can fully concentrate without other distractions. Many a decision has been finally reached, or hitherto unexpressed emotions unfolded to each other, during the tranquillity of an English country walk.

Although Nick has confessed to feeling somewhat helpless in trying to support me over the years, I have assured him that his constant love, sympathy and astonishing patience when I am finding life difficult, and am perhaps not very pleasant to live with, are profoundly helpful. His listening ear, practical kindnesses and comforting arms usually go further than a theological treatise! But of course I do also greatly appreciate his ability and help in applying Scripture to our circumstances. Nick's solid faith has always been a great example to me, and some of his recent sermons in church have been absolutely pivotal in helping me to rethink our situation in a more God-honouring manner. I am deeply thankful to God for the husband He has given me in Nick.

Thankfully, we have also been able to respect each other's conscience about fertility treatments. We have tried to reassure each other in many ways of our continuing love for and commitment to each other, while also being truthful about our disappointment, our lack, and how this trial of infertility has affected us negatively, as a couple. Sometimes we have needed to be very honest with each other about how we are coping with each other's responses and behaviour, or those of other people, to our situation. We have tried to encourage each other when very down, and even gently rebuke each other, if necessary. We try to remember that God, in His wisdom, has taken us both, as a couple, *together* into this trial of infertility. We try not to use our pain as an excuse for sinful behaviour with each other. We have also tried to focus on any 'positive' aspects of our situation that we have been able to acknowledge so far, such as being able to have evenings out and nights away, just the two of us, without ever needing to sort out childcare. It is also good to remind ourselves regularly that, despite any struggles and disillusionment during the pressures of infertility, sex is one of God's good gifts to us as couples. Whether or not it will ever result in conception, it binds us closer to each other and should not be neglected.

We remember, and thankfully have been able to reassure each other, that we did not marry for the sole purpose of having children. Even though we had very much hoped to have a family, we married because we loved each other and wanted to be together. Now after fourteen years of marriage, and despite the grief of our childlessness which has so indelibly shaped our experience together, we still have many other happy memories and praise God for all He has given us, and the way He has used us together in His service. (I will expand on this a little more later.)

However, as with everything else in our Christian lives, we have had to work hard at all of the above; it does not just happen naturally. We have tried to keep up praying together about this and other issues in our lives. We have to rely completely on God for empowering through His Holy Spirit. We also often need to ask for forgiveness from each other, and develop forgiving spirits ourselves.

Surely this can even become the experience for those who perhaps did initially marry only to have children. Perhaps some couples feel their problems are really beyond them, and they may benefit from some caring Christian counselling (I have added details of a suitable network in

Appendix 1). Perhaps it might also help some couples to develop a good, mutually supportive and trusting friendship with another Christian couple, not necessarily childless themselves, in which problems can be shared and prayed through.

I am encouraged by another short paragraph from Katherine Hall. She clearly envisages hope for the present, and future, in childless marriages:

> If love can persist through the strain of childlessness, then surely this is a good marriage ... A marriage, which though disappointed, can still remain good and unbitter, with shared pleasure, mutual respect and deepening trust, will be an unusually strong one, though its strength may not become apparent until the late years, the years when many marriages collapse because the joint interest of child rearing is now over. The childless marriage is unlikely to crumble at this late stage, if the couple have already faced each other across the chasm of emptiness and found in each other a source of richness.[1]

Pause for thought

- How is the Lord answering the prayer you wrote at the end of Chapter 4?
- How can you refocus your marriage right now?
- Write down three things the Lord has done in your lives through this painful experience.

Bible passages for reflection

Love is patient, love is kind. It does not envy, it does not boast, it is not proud. It is not rude, it is not self-seeking, it is not easily angered, it keeps no record of wrongs. Love does not delight in evil but rejoices with the truth. It always protects, always trusts, always hopes, always perseveres. Love never fails. (1 Cor. 13:4–8a)

Two are better than one,
  because they have a good return for their work:
If one falls down,
  his friend can help him up.
But pity the man who falls
  and has no one to help him up!
Also, if two lie down together, they will keep warm.
  But how can one keep warm alone?
Though one may be overpowered,
  two can defend themselves.
A cord of three strands is not quickly broken. (Eccles. 4:9–12)

Prayer

Father, we praise you for your wonderful gift to us of marriage. Thank you for the love and joy we share together. You design marriage to be a reflection of the intimate and loving relationship between Christ and His church. Thank you that this reflection is not marred by the absence of any children. But keep us from spoiling it by our sin. We know the devil tries to ruin our marriage—but Jesus is stronger! Give us patience with each other, and slowness to anger, especially when we feel the pain and stress of our situation. Help us to be open, 'naked' with each other, as we share our concerns, feelings and struggles. Draw us closer to yourself and to each other as we come to you together in prayer. Help us to love and care for each other as you desire, and as we promised on our wedding day, for better and for worse. Equip and strengthen us with your grace, so that our marriage might reflect ever more deeply the joy and wonder of relationship with Jesus. In His name, Amen.

Recognizing that others hurt too

Infertility can become such an all-consuming problem that we may forget one simple truth: others also suffer in this life. We can sometimes be tempted to think that nobody else suffers as we do, with our own unique perplexity of painful circumstances: all the countless 'little hurts' which combine into one great whole. Yet in dealing with my own childlessness I have become aware of others with this very problem; those who have been, or are, struggling equally, perhaps even more. For example, I am grateful we do not live in a society or during an era when infertility is total social anathema. We think of biblical women like Sarah, Rachel and Elizabeth, who rejoiced, '[The Lord] has taken away my disgrace' when after many years of childlessness they gave birth to their sons. In biblical times infertility was considered to be a sign of God's disfavour or even judgement on a couple, and, especially, it seems, on the woman. Isaiah 54:1, although actually describing Israel as a nation, nevertheless implies that 'barren women' were often thought of as 'desolate' (or 'deserted'). This heart-breaking word was used to describe women without the protection and status of a husband. For the childless woman, this may have been so because her husband had discarded her. 'Desolate' was also used of the beautiful Tamar, daughter of King David, after she had been violated and then rejected by her half-brother Amnon in 2 Samuel 13. The word suggests being a hopeless outcast, unwanted, unmarriageable, and considered to be of little value.

I am aware that even today some cultures around the world condone easy abandonment (or worse) of a childless wife. Some infertile wives, although not entirely cast off, may be degraded to a considerably lower status, all favour being given to a newer, fertile wife. Other societies actually practise humiliating rituals on childless couples at community weddings or social gatherings, which leave them bruised and aching inside for a long time. Once again, I thank God that I have been preserved from such cruelty myself. One friend of ours recalls a very young woman who, many years ago, sat alongside her in a fertility clinic, also waiting for results. This girl obviously came from a different cultural background, one that sets great store on the producing of children, especially sons. There could have been horrible repercussions for her if she were found to be permanently infertile. Our friend remembers, 'I will never forget the look of complete and utter terror on her face.'

In the aftermath of our miscarriage, another local pastor's wife came to comfort me. I was sharing how shattered and lonely I felt, and that there seemed to be no one else in my position. She then sensitively shared with me about a family member of hers who had also lost a baby at about the same time as us. After describing this woman's experience, which was also awful, she reassured me, 'So you see, Sarah, you are *not* alone.' Her very loving and concerned manner helped me feel understood. She wisely did not compare our situations, or in any way imply that I was suffering less than her relative; but she helped me feel less isolated. Perhaps just as importantly, however, I also became personally grateful to God that I had not had to suffer certain very painful aspects of that other situation.

We do not have the monopoly on pain

I cannot remember now where I encountered the above pithy little statement, but it has stuck in my mind for years. Lois Flowers very helpfully reminds infertile people that, although our struggles may be heart-rending, unusual and prolonged, perhaps even ranking as one of life's biggest 'injustices', other people (not necessarily infertile) also suffer horrendously. Perhaps we can forget that sometimes, in the midst of everything. But over the years, as I have watched the news, read, learned about and shared other people's lives, I have come to thank God wholeheartedly that he has kept certain dreadful experiences out of my life. It has spurred us on to pray for those who are in unimaginable circumstances.

In our own family-centred society (and, as has also been noted, *churches*), there are many different people who can feel left out in the cold because they do not fit into the 'happy family' category for their age group. I am grateful to God when he has gently directed my attention to the sufferings of these others, whatever the problems may be. Being so utterly broken over our infertility and miscarriage has helped me feel more compassion for people who hurt in different ways. It has helped me to remember that many people experience bereavement and disappointment, whether it be through the death of a loved one, singleness, relationship breakdown, violation through an attack, long-term illness or fall-out from an accident, redundancy, repeated failure and many other trials. I realize that all of these can result in the same desperate numb pain, the wondering how life can go on or ever be the same again.

We also realize that there are others whose experience of parenthood itself results in terrible sadness. It would be hard to forget the shock and depths of grief brought to my whole family when my little brother died. I have often wondered how it must be as a parent to watch in hopelessness at the bedside of a dearly loved but desperately sick child, or to lose an older child, perhaps even in their adulthood. It must be utterly heart-rending to receive the terrible diagnosis that an accident, illness or genetic inheritance has caused permanent damage to a precious child. Furthermore, we have sat with older Christian parents, some of them also in the ministry, listening to descriptions of how their much-loved and much-prayed-for children have crushed their hearts through rebellion or appalling actions with life-long consequences. One friend poignantly revealed, 'I have cried more tears over my children than over anything else.' Of course, an infertile woman may well have cried more tears so far over her infertility than over anything else, and probably nothing will ever stop her desiring children of her own. We always hope for the best. But I have found it profoundly helpful to consider how parenting itself can bring untold heartache for some, as well as the joy which we often focus upon solely. We are thankful to God for sparing us some of that particular pain so far.

The grass is not always greener

It is always easy to think that life would be so much happier if we just had that one thing we really want so much. But it simply does not always work that way, does it? I try to remind myself of this when perhaps my misery causes me to lose perspective. I have recently begun to observe more closely how for some couples the responsibilities, anxieties and demands of family life, despite bringing much joy, can also be utterly overwhelming, challenging and exhausting. It really cannot be easy to raise children in our increasingly materialistic, immoral and unsafe society. There are so many important decisions to be made for the children, and I have seen how difficult it can sometimes be to make the right ones. Furthermore, many people have discovered themselves to be in a situation of lone parenthood when that was far from their expectations and hopes. Additionally, although the childless may fear being alone and lonely in the years ahead, I have recently observed with sadness that there are many aged men and women with children of their own yet who are, for various reasons, also isolated in their old age. Having children is really no guarantee of future security and happiness. That is surely found in God alone.

If I am so dissatisfied now, what makes me think that all my problems will disappear if God gives me a child? Perhaps then I will have other heartaches. Is it not also possible that having a baby *may not* ultimately make me as happy and relaxed as I currently imagine it will? We so often think only about the positives when longing and endlessly praying for a family. King Hezekiah's story is something of a warning for us here. In 2 Kings 20 we see how this godly king was on the point of death but begged the Lord with bitter tears and anguish for healing. It seems he could not face the prospect of death just then, and he cited his righteous conduct as a reason for God to answer positively. God did of course answer Hezekiah and gave him an extra fifteen years of life. But our warning is that they were evidently not fruitful years, and Hezekiah eventually died with the sad knowledge of bad times ahead for his family. We do not always know what will be best for us in this life. But God does.

I have also recently begun to realize that those who have little ones to care for suffer much more when they try to protect them in situations of natural disaster and intense persecution. Jesus himself made a shocking statement in Luke 23:29 as he foresaw the imminent fall of Jerusalem in AD 70. He prophesied that those days would be so appalling that *childless* ('barren') women would become the ones considered 'blessed'. This was revolutionary indeed for that family-centred society, and history proved AD 70 to be exactly the tragedy Jesus had foretold. In our bleakest times, Nick and I find it helpful to focus on, help and pray for other Christians who are suffering now, among those we know personally, but also those in very different contexts around the world. Reading missionary biographies,

Operation World, or scanning the literature of organizations like Christian Solidarity Worldwide reminds us of how harrowing are the lives of many other people. Some are enduring unspeakable circumstances that we in the West are privileged not to know. Some Christian women have watched in helplessness as beloved husbands and children have been arrested, imprisoned or worse in front of their eyes, simply for being faithful to the Lord. They too are in need of much support. These considerations help us turn our thoughts away from our own sufferings, even temporarily, and also cause us to remember God's 'bigger picture': how this world is not our final home, and our lives are actually just one small piece of His much greater, and eventually glorious, 'whole'.

Pause for thought

- In what ways does the Lord sympathize with you as your great High Priest?
- How has your own pain and suffering given you empathy for others?
- How might the Lord be preparing you for a ministry to others who are suffering pain, hurt, loss or grief?

Bible passages for reflection

Near the cross of Jesus stood his mother, his mother's sister, Mary the wife of Clopas, and Mary Magdalene. When Jesus saw his mother there, and the disciple whom he loved standing near by, he said to his mother, 'Dear woman, here is your son,' and to the disciple, 'Here is your mother.' From that time on, this disciple took her into his home. (John 19:25–27)

... Mourn with those who mourn. (Rom. 12:15b)

Prayer

O God and Father of our Lord Jesus Christ, you sent your Son into this world to be made flesh, so that He might be made complete through His sufferings. He has been tested in every way as we are, by the various pains He endured, and He understands what is involved when we suffer. So you understand why I so easily get absorbed by and obsessed with my own sufferings, and why my pain hinders me from looking outwards. I confess that at times I've been unable to see any further than myself and my own problems. Forgive me for when that has meant I've been negligent in showing love and care to others who suffer. Lift my eyes to see that others go through their own trials and difficulties. I remember that Jesus, in the depths of His unimaginable suffering on the cross, yet turned His attention to His mother's needs. Grant me a Christlike concern for others in need. Help me, where I can, to give them something of the practical love and prayer support which I desire for myself. In the name of Jesus, Amen.

Developing thankful hearts

As mentioned before, many infertile couples believe that nothing else in life could ever be so exciting or fulfilling as becoming pregnant, giving birth to a baby and raising a family of their own. However, as Christians we cannot ignore the fact that the Bible commands us to 'be content' (Heb. 13:5) and to 'Give thanks in *all* circumstances' (1 Thes. 5:18, my italics). Nick and I have discovered that it is possible, even in infertility, to learn this. It has been, and still is, a very slow process, one we could not even have begun without the Lord's help.

One way in which Nick and I have been helped in developing contentment is by constantly reminding ourselves of all the good things God *has* blessed us with. We would not have chosen our childless situation, but we do believe that children are a gift, not a 'right', and we can see that God has greatly privileged us in other ways, with other blessings, some of which seem even to be unique to us as a couple. We realize that there are many others who would be grateful to have everything that we enjoy. We are beginning again, albeit very slowly, to be grateful for the life God has given us, without continuing to hanker after what He has not given. He has given us much that can bring pleasure in this life, and I find it helpful to focus on that. I do believe that Nick and I are finally beginning to rediscover some glimmers of excitement at our remaining future on earth. Who knows what God has planned?

Here are some of our blessings and privileges—though this is not by any means an exhaustive list.

Thankful for practical blessings

God has blessed most of us in the West with material abundance we should not take for granted. Many people in other parts of the world, or at other times in history, do or did not experience this, and probably could not even imagine the wealth and facilities we now enjoy. Among many other blessings Nick and I are personally thankful for is the fact that we live in a country which is usually at peace, replete with general law and order, which has a National Health Service, many other social benefits, and, as yet, freedom of speech. We are thankful that we have a lovely home with modern conveniences, good quality and quantity of clothing and food, enough money to cover necessities and more, interesting holidays, opportunities to travel in this and other parts of the world, a car, the health and physical fitness to be able to experience God's amazing creation, plenty of books, films and music for our enjoyment, a good education and interesting work. Getting involved in a new practical project at church, work or in the home and garden can be a real tonic when struggling with infertility depression, and I am thankful for the ability to do such things.

One friend who is waiting for a pregnancy recently emailed me about planning for and seeking new avenues of employment. She needed to know what God would have her do. Did she perhaps need to take a step sideways in her work? She wrote, 'Wouldn't it be much easier if the "family course" were in front of us to follow. But it is not … and we need to "think outside the box" because God has put us outside the box.' Her words resonated with me, of course. However, I also considered how blessed women are who live in countries like ours where there are so many varied opportunities for participation in interesting training courses and in paid or voluntary work inside and outside the home.

Likewise, Nick and I have discovered that it is better to make plans (perhaps for that once-in-a-lifetime visit to missionaries abroad) rather than constantly put things off, hoping for a pregnancy. Far better to cancel later for a joyful reason, if need be, than be left with further regrets at the end of a year for things not done, and still to have no children. Sometimes I have even been able to say to myself, 'Well, if we did have children, we wouldn't have been able to do this …'

Thankful for special people

I have already described how we have enjoyed outstanding support through faithful and loving family and friends, and the children of our friends, who have brought us much happiness and often distraction from our sadness.

We also have, at the time of writing, five nephews and a niece, plus another on the way, and they too have brought us much interest and joy. We love them, and we love seeing them grow up. On Mother's and Fathers' Days especially we thank God for our own wonderful parents and the devoted care they have shown us throughout our lives. That is something for us to be ever grateful for on the countless Mother's and Father's Days which may still stretch ahead of us.

Also, of course, we have each other. We are blessed to be in a marriage which, despite our trials, has been happy for many years. A childless pastor's wife I know has learned to be content in her situation partly because she believes their marriage to be closer than those of many fertile couples she knows. They would not have initially chosen childlessness, but they now have more time to support and care for each other in the demands of their life. Strangely, perhaps, I was once helped by a couple in a church who revealed to me that they had no children because they had never wanted any. I never discovered the reasons behind their decision, but they were highly positive about their situation, and encouraged me that there was so much we could do without children. Even though I found it hard to relate to their choice at the time, it did help me to begin glimpsing a life beyond infertility, and to consider that having children is actually not everything in life.

Nick and I are deeply grateful for having been members of good churches with caring and wise church leaders over the years, together with the wonderful congregation we now serve. It was a privilege to study at Bible college for two years, as it is to enjoy freedom of worship openly and to have at our fingertips a wealth of good Christian resources written by knowledgeable, godly Christians. We are thankful, too, for all the other ways God has used us in His service over the years, knowing that this has been His plan for our lives so far. There are some individuals, both in church contexts and elsewhere, whom we would certainly not have been able to reach so effectively if we already had children. We are also thankful for the ways in which God has involved us in the lives of other people's children, myself through teaching and both of us in the church fellowships we have known. We are thankful for the opportunities He has given us to develop creativity and hospitality in our home, even without the children we have wanted so much. Our house may be devoid of our own offspring, but it is peaceful and a refuge for us. Not only that, but it is happily full when we invite friends, relatives and other families over. We love it when they burst through the front door, any youngsters heading straight for the old wooden chest in the sitting room. All those cherished books, toys and games kept from our own childhoods have found a use!

Thankful for spiritual blessings

A struggling infertile couple may not always be able to see their blessings, let alone count them, and of course the physical and relational blessings will differ with each couple. Our own list of those blessings may not match that of others very well at all. But even within the sadness of infertility, we need to remember that we all still have much to thank our gracious God for—especially for all the spiritual blessings we have received as Christians, through Jesus. Our freedom in Christ and His salvation is always a reality for us, whatever else we do or do not have. It really helps me if I remind myself that, as a sinner who initially rejected God, I did not actually deserve anything from Him at all. Yet for us who now know Jesus, we are not only redeemed from sin and shame, but we have been given so much more in this life as well. Supremely, we know forgiveness, and peace with God as His adopted and dearly loved children. We have been washed clean from all our impurities, and have been given the Holy Spirit to help us resist evil and live lives that please God. We have Jesus as our faithful Friend through all the storms of life; He is the 'friend who sticks closer than a brother' (Prov. 18:24). If we are in any doubt about all the spiritual privileges we have been given through Jesus, or if our trial has caused us to lose our joy, it may help to do a detailed study of Ephesians 1. This can help us to remember all that God has done and will do for us, and to be thankful to Him again (Some of the themes it contains will be explored later in this book.)

Sometimes, when I meditate on the cross and all that Jesus did for me there, sacrificially laying down His very life that I might know heaven for eternity and peace in the here and now, I wonder how I can doubt His love. I admit it has taken me a long time to learn to think in this way. It is still so easy to take things for granted, or to think that the pain of infertility blots out all our other blessings.

Thankful for new God-given opportunities

To be honest, I do not like to apply the description 'infertile'—or even 'barren'—to Nick and myself. Even if technically correct, they seem such negative words (as does 'sterile'). I actually prefer the politically correct term 'non-parents'! But even that can seem a little empty. 'Child-free' was suggested by Beth Spring and that, perhaps, has far more positive connotations. You see, we are deeply encouraged and thankful to observe in our other 'infertile' friends that a biologically childless marriage may yet become abundantly fruitful in many other areas. This is especially obvious in those who have been living with childlessness for many years. As one of these friends wrote recently, part of the successful grieving and healing process for her and her husband meant 're-investing the energy invested in what was lost into other important areas'. And this they have done very well. It is quite clear from observing such couples that God did not institute marriage simply for the purpose of producing biological children. There are many other ways in which infertile couples are clearly 'right' for each other and can serve God. For example, Nick and I have discovered over the years that our particular personality match, together with our unique knowledge of each other's thought processes, makes us an excellent team for speaking with people at church and conversing in evangelistic situations. We complement each other, and are highly encouraged about this. As Genesis 1:28 teaches, all people are called to 'subdue', or manage, the earth. Along these lines, we also know many single, childless individuals who live highly interesting, useful and God-honouring lives.

To give just a few examples aside from useful paid employment, we know childless people who have ministered through the loving adoption or fostering of needy children, some of whom came from the most distressing of backgrounds. We know others who are excellent at evangelism and outreach, or who contribute faithfully to many aspects of church life, community life or children's work. There are those who open their peaceful homes with generous hospitality, some who are abundantly creative, energetic and healthy, others who have much time to devote to very vulnerable people, especially, perhaps, to those who do not 'fit' well into society. Yet others are counsellors, or can commit more time and resources to encouraging and assisting their family members, despondent Christians or struggling missionaries.

After our initial diagnosis of infertility, I received a compassionate letter from an old friend. Not a biological mother herself, she reminded me that many childless Christians yet have 'spiritual children'. These are those, young and old, with whom they have spent much time, love and energy to introduce to, or nurture in, the Christian faith. What is more, these 'spiritual children' will be there alongside them in heaven. My friend had faithfully run a girls' Bible class for over forty years and I had been a member of this. We are thankful for the fine examples of some of these other childless Christians. As we watch them, God graciously gives us so much encouragement to live a full and productive life!

Perhaps if we are struggling to find practical outlets for our talents and love we may need to pray that God will open the right nurturing opportunities to us. Lois, a friend currently struggling with infertility, also realizes that this circumstance is a burden that God has 'privileged us to bear'. She recently suggested, 'Perhaps someone else would not be able to cope as well with it ... Despite our enormous struggles we may eventually find the strength to speak out about it, and help others, where someone else would not be confident enough to do so.' Along these lines Lois has written a paper entitled 'Godly Discontentment?' It includes thoughts on how we can respond in a godly manner to this undesired situation of infertility. Early on in the paper she particularly emphasizes the aching difficulties she has experienced in childlessness, especially the loose emotions and lack of fulfilment resulting from her grief, some of which I described in Chapter 2. But Lois finishes her paper with this encouragement:

> The emotions which one has need to be found a home, a vent, and a positive outlet. The word 'contentment' is there in Scripture alongside the words 'contend', 'struggle', 'fight'. These are not passive words with little energy attached. The 'unsettled' and vagrant emotions which one feels at the loss can be channelled and directed into contending, striving, struggling, fighting, to bring about a positive end ... into a just and worthy cause.[1]

Pause for thought

- Can you list ten ways in which the Lord has blessed you spiritually and materially?
- Can you list six ways in which the Lord is using this unique, though unwanted, situation of childlessness for His glory in your life?
- Pray about any particular ministries that are open to you because of your situation and seek God's plan for you to be involved with one of these.
- Pray for fruitfulness in this potential new area of ministry.

Bible passages for reflection

Enter his gates with thanksgiving
  and his courts with praise;
  give thanks to him and praise his name.
For the LORD is good and his love endures for ever;
  his faithfulness continues through all generations. (Ps. 100:4–5)

But thanks be to God, who always leads us in triumphal procession in Christ and through us spreads everywhere the fragrance of the knowledge of him. (2 Cor. 2:14)

Thanks be to God for his indescribable gift! (2 Cor. 9:15)

Prayer

Loving Father, you are good and kind. Goodness and kindness describe your nature, and in particular you are good to your children. You have been good to me in so many different ways. You have shown me your lovingkindness, and have showered blessing upon blessing on me. Thank you. Father, you know that at times I have been so blinded by my tears and pain that I have lost sight of all your goodness. In your mercy, forgive my ingratitude. Please guide my thoughts and open my eyes to see the multitude of ways in which you have been good to me, to recognize the many good gifts you have given me, and to contemplate the awesomely rich spiritual blessings I have in Christ. Help me to understand how little I deserve from you. Create in me a thankful heart that focuses less on what I lack and is simply grateful to you for all that I have—that you might receive all the praise and glory. Amen.

Finding specific help in God's Word

In times of desperation and bleakest despair it has been our main lifeline to recall and apply spiritual truth from the Bible. Nick and I have discovered this has come from our own study of Scripture, but also through sermons and books, or conversations with each other, family and friends.

The Bible assures us that we are greatly loved by God, more than we will ever be able to comprehend, and He has promised us, as Christians, a glorious future ahead. The struggle may be tremendously hard. As mentioned before, I am often in need of relearning these lessons. Sometimes truths that once shone brightly and helped so much have become dim. This is especially so when a new wave of disappointment, confusion or pain threatens to sweep us away or causes us to spiral downwards again. When this happens Lydia Brownback urges us to think in this way:

> All God does in our lives and everywhere he leads us has one overarching purpose, which is to deepen our relationship with him and to further his glory through us … A heartfelt grasp of God's primary purpose will enable us to enjoy his secondary blessings and also to live contentedly with those we lack.[1]

It certainly seems to be true that the more we have immersed ourselves in God's Word, the better able we have been to apply this knowledge when our hearts have been hurting. Scripture helps us think positively again when we have become trapped in a negative mindset. Although we have been set back in unforeseen ways by our miscarriage, the truth Nick and I had slowly learned in the previous nine years of infertility has helped in navigating the trauma. We have been taught countless truths about our amazing God. We thank Him for His enabling thus far. The following is some of what we have learned.

God has a wonderful character

As described in Chapter 1, our infertility and miscarriage experience has often caused me to doubt, and to wonder, 'Is God really in control of my life at all? For that matter, is He in control of any of the heartaches and devastation that people suffer?' We live in a fallen world and infertility is, as we have considered, just one aspect of the entire tapestry of human suffering down the ages. If God loves me, why has He not, in His power, changed or prevented my struggles? Is it actually because He cannot? Has He actually any control over who conceives and who does not? We can begin to doubt if God really is good, loving and powerful.

The Bible assures us throughout that no matter how it may seem to us, God is indeed in control of the entire universe: that He planned and created it, that He is intimately involved with every aspect of its working, and that He has the entire story of human history and, most importantly, His salvation plan worked out from beginning to end. He is bringing this 'big picture' to pass. Not only that, but He also plans the life story for each individual human being. He watched closely and formed us as we developed in our mothers' wombs (Ps. 139 again). For many years I have loved the 'Divine Weaver' poem (see Appendix 2). It speaks so beautifully of God's mysterious workings in the life of a Christian, and of how it all has a wonderful purpose which will one day be revealed.

So we know, then, that every conception that does *or does not* occur is under God's watchful eye and control. It is not random. As considered earlier, God's providence also includes any congenital problems rendering us infertile or challenged in other areas of life. Those millions of little lives which have been miscarried are surely therefore under His control as well. We are also told throughout Scripture of our God's strength, power and ability to save. The verses are too numerous to mention all of them here, but the Psalms are a good place to start. Nowhere does the Bible ever tell us that God has been too weak to remedy a situation, that something slipped His notice or that He made a mistake. It is quite the reverse.

But if we accept that God *is* in control, does that then make Him guilty of favouritism, neglect, cruelty or lack of care towards certain Christians? Can we think such things? As Nick once reminded me from a sermon he had heard, 'Remember that *God* is *good* and *Satan* is *bad*. Never get the two confused.' Scripture teaches throughout that God is perfect, more holy than we sinful beings can ever understand. This is emphasized, for example, in Leviticus 11:44 and then echoed in 1 Peter 1:15–16: 'Be holy, *because I am holy*' (my italics). This teaches us that God, being completely pure and righteous, will never do anything wrong; He will never do anything unjust, hurtful or cruel. He will never trifle with or mock our feelings. He will never bring anything upon us just to 'get' us. One of the earliest great biblical descriptions of God's wonderful and righteous character is found in Exodus 34:6 and begins thus: 'The LORD, the LORD, the compassionate and gracious God, slow to anger, abounding in love and faithfulness, maintaining love to thousands, and forgiving wickedness, rebellion and sin.'

I find it helpful to recall and meditate on such verses especially when struggling with doubts over God's character. Some of my friends find it beneficial to write down verses like these and stick them in obvious places around the home, as it helps to memorize them.

As we see in Job chapters 1 and 2, it is actually Satan, the father of lies, who hates us and wishes to destroy us. Likewise, 1 Peter 5:8 warns us, 'Be self-controlled and alert. Your enemy the devil prowls around like a roaring lion looking for someone to devour.' Satan and our sinful, fallen world are the ultimate cause of all that hurts us, but he would yet deceive us into believing that it is God's fault. We may think we are being hurt in every possible way we could be in our infertility, struggling with events that seem designed to cause us maximum pain. But the Bible assures us that it is not because *God* is cruel.

Sometimes, when I am finding life very hard, I simply remind myself, 'God is in control, and God is good.' But I have also found that when I focus on Jesus, discovering more of Him in the Bible, especially in the Gospels, everything else falls into place. Jesus, who is both God and man, shows us exactly who God is and what He is like. Jesus Christ demonstrates that:

- God is concerned for all people and treats them all with fairness;
- He knows and loves all people individually, and gives appropriate help to each situation;
- He is concerned for those who feel sidelined by society;

- He has compassion on the sick, the poor and all other needy, desperate people;
- He puts wrongs right;
- He is powerful in people's lives, over the forces of nature, over Satan and every evil being;
- He is deeply angry at wickedness and injustice;
- He bears with us and helps us in our weaknesses;
- He speaks wisdom into every situation;
- He aches and cries with us in our deepest pain, for He has been there.

We are not alone. He understands how it feels to be mocked or humiliated, misunderstood, frustrated, deeply disappointed, totally isolated and utterly broken. He gives peace where there has been turmoil. He promises those who turn to Him undeserved forgiveness and joy unspeakable, for ever. He has the power to help us in all our weakness.

Throughout the Gospels we see unfolded to us this wonderful person of Jesus Christ. And He is God. *Our* God! How can we *not* trust Him?

Our identity and worth are found in God

In the Sermon on the Mount in Matthew 6:19 Jesus warned us about putting our hope in earthly blessings or treasures. He said, 'Do not store up for yourselves treasures on earth, where moth and rust destroy, and where thieves break in and steal.'

Usually the treasure we envisage Jesus to be speaking about is money or worldly possessions. But could He not also be talking about *all* our other earthly 'treasures', including our sense of status in life, physical strengths and natural abilities, occupations and much-loved family members: that (and those) which endows us with our core sense of identity and self-worth? Perhaps some of us gain our sense of identity through being a husband or wife, son or daughter, friend, church worker, teacher, doctor or pastor: the list is endless. But we know that all these 'treasures' could be stripped away from us, perhaps including the *dream* of a family of our own. Should such a tragedy happen, where would that leave us?

You may remember how for me, one deeply perplexing aspect of my infertility has been the struggle to establish my core identity: who or what I am, as I have no children. Am I to be defined purely and for ever as a 'childless mother'? How do we resolve our identity crisis when treasured hopes for the future pattern of our lives have never materialized? Jesus continued in Matthew 6:20–21: 'But store up for yourselves treasures in heaven, where moth and rust do not destroy, and where thieves do not break in and steal. For where your treasure is, there your heart will be also.' Jesus is urging us to place the entirety of our lives into his hands, and to remember that this life is not all there is. All humanity is made in God's image (Gen. 1:27), we are His creatures, and that is fundamental to our identity and intrinsic worth as human beings. But those of us who are Christians, who have accepted Christ's death on our behalf, rediscover on a deeper level our core identity and status in being the much-loved *children* of God who are in relationship with Him. Although I had not thought in much detail at the time, the rather faltering definition of my identity which finally emerged in that long-ago Bible study was correct: I am first and foremost a child of God. We Christians are children of the King! We are of infinite worth: adopted, treasured and valued by Him. If we revel in being God's children and if we live first and foremost to please Him, whatever our circumstances, our joy in this *and* the next life will be great. We must not let the painful circumstances of this present life pull us away from this foundational truth. Being sons and daughters of the supreme and living God gives our lives dignity, meaning and purpose. Whatever our appearance or health, whatever we have or do not have (including children of our own), whatever we can or cannot do, whatever our successes or failures, we are, and always will be, children of the King. Our practical purpose day by day, and throughout the remainder of our earthly lives, is, therefore, to serve our loving heavenly Father in the ways He has wisely decided for us. As I am living the life that God has marked out for me, as a follower of Christ, it is therefore primarily what *God* thinks of me and what I do that matters, rather than what other people think I should or should not be doing.

Amazingly, we recognize that God lovingly and compassionately planned our life's pathway even before we were conceived! Consider how He encouraged the prophet Jeremiah: 'Before I formed you in the womb I knew you, before you were born I set you apart' (Jer. 1:5). Despite how we may sometimes be tempted to think the opposite, Bible passages such as these again assure us that our lives and experiences, even infertility, are not random accidents. God loved us and chose us for Himself, to be His holy children. Just how precious we are as these children of the King is underlined when the apostle Paul declares that this choice was made even 'before the creation of the world' (Eph. 1:4).

This rediscovery of my core identity was a significant milestone in my infertility journey, just as it was for a friend. Perhaps you can recall her concern (described in Chapter 10) as she sat in the hospital waiting room, watching the young girl who was simply terrified at the possible implications of her infertility. At that moment the amazing security we have as Christians was brought home to my friend. She says, 'I realized how blessed we are to know that our worth does not come from our desires being met, our physical functioning ability, giving birth to children, or any other earthly status, but entirely from *being a child of God*.'

The Old Testament prophet Habakkuk describes utter physical desolation and barrenness. Such is the life of someone who does not seem to be experiencing anything much in the way of worldly prosperity, success or status. In what would he find his identity? Only through his relationship with God:

> Though the fig-tree does not bud
>   and there are no grapes on the vines,
> though the olive crop fails
>   and the fields produce no food,
> though there are no sheep in the pen
>   and no cattle in the stalls,
> yet I will rejoice in the LORD,
>   I will be joyful in God my Saviour.
> The Sovereign LORD is my strength;
>   he makes my feet like the feet of a deer,
>   he enables me to go on the heights.
>
> (Hab. 3:17–19)

Although our circumstances may hurt us, we continue to trust and obey our heavenly Father, in whom we find our true identity. Thus we lay up our 'treasures'.

Strange as it may seem, Nick and I have also found it helpful to consider a few of the harder truths that God's Word teaches us, even in the pain of our childlessness.

Happiness is not promised in this life

Despite much forceful teaching in some circles of the Christian church, Jesus never said or even implied that life would be easy for His faithful people. He does not assure us that coming to trust in Him will result in a carefree end to all our troubles. In fact, for many Christians, it seems their experience is quite the opposite.

As we are painfully aware, the whole world is fallen and groaning in agony, and it is the common lot of humans everywhere to suffer in many ways. We as Christians are not exempt from any of this suffering. We need only to look at the experiences of God's faithful people throughout Scripture and down the ages since to see this. As non-Christians and Christians alike suffer debilitating illnesses, lose their loved ones (perhaps even all their children), suffer in catastrophes or from crime, are disappointed in many ways, are lonely, hungry, homeless or depressed, so others of us are infertile. God does not necessarily promise to remove such pain from us in our time on this earth—not even from His much-loved children. Indeed, we have considered that as Christians there are often extra dimensions to our sufferings which can compound our difficulties, such as persecution, temptation and seemingly unanswered prayers. Jesus Himself emphasized, 'In this world you will have trouble' (John 16:33).

Not only that, but when God responded to the first human sin in Genesis, one of the dreadful consequences for Eve and her female descendants was, 'I will greatly increase your pains in childbearing' (Gen. 3:16). A friend who has suffered several miscarriages suggested that this could perhaps apply to every aspect concerning this fundamental area of women's lives. Problems conceiving, miscarriage, ectopic pregnancies, stillbirths, very difficult deliveries when the lives of mother and baby hang in the balance or are even lost: is this not all part of that ancient warning to Eve? We still live in the same world and still suffer the dire results of the fall. God has not promised that we will all have children, or that everything will turn out well if we do.

I wonder if it is harder now in the materialistic West than ever before to accept this truth. Perhaps we have all imbibed to some extent the philosophy urging us that we can have everything we want, whenever we want it. For example, with infertility—and indeed with any other medical problem—we often do not anticipate being told, 'I'm sorry, but there's just nothing we can do for you.' We expect resolutions to our difficulties in this technologically advanced age. We can even think, albeit subconsciously, that we have an entitlement to such. It is an achingly hard lesson to learn through a painful trial like infertility, but the fact is that we do *not* always get what we want in this present life. Sometimes we actually do have to take 'no' for an answer! In contrast to the secular training we may have received in our childhood and teenage years, we may need eventually to accept that it is not always possible to realize our hopes and dreams in the here and now. The dream of raising our own family may be extinguished quite suddenly, or may slowly fade until we know for sure it has gone for ever, but for some of us the certainty is that it will never happen. Not all of our longings may be satisfied in this life. We also know that the Bible tells us that we cannot demand such privileges from God. It is His world, and we are His created beings. Children are His gifts! As emphasized before, they are not a right or even a human achievement, no matter how they may sometimes be seen. I confess that often I just long for the pleasant blessings God gives and am sometimes very reluctant to accept the pain He also allows. Perhaps we are all like that to some extent?

We see God's control of fertility clearly demonstrated when couples are told by doctors that their chances of conceiving naturally are virtually zero—but then they do just that, and even sometimes go on to raise a good-sized family. Wonderful and encouraging as this is, as mentioned previously, it can also be perplexing to infertile couples like ourselves who have nothing wrong diagnosed with them and yet do not conceive. But Nick and I have found it important to take note of these very situations, because it has shown us once again that it is God who is ultimately in control of conception, not human beings. And God knows what each person needs.

Is infertility a judgement?

As mentioned above, some people will try to convince us that the Christian life should be one of perpetual health, wealth and happiness. They may declare that if this is not so for an individual, there is something wrong with that person's faith, or that they must be entrenched in some dreadful sin; perhaps they are undergoing punishment for this sin. Concerning infertility and miscarriage in particular they may use Bible texts such as verses in Exodus 23 and 2 Samuel 6 to justify their views. While our experience and our hearts tell us that surely such an extrapolation cannot always be right, I will admit that these are passages which for many years left me as an infertile woman feeling very uncomfortable and, when they were read in public at church, very embarrassed. Therefore it is worth looking in more detail at these Scriptures in their original contexts, and certainly before we start suggesting that they condemn any couple today.

The historical context of Exodus 23:25–31 records God confirming His covenant with Israel through instructions to Moses. It is a beautiful passage which reveals the loving heart of God for His chosen people and His desire for them as a nation to live fulfilled and fruitful lives in every respect. Although they lived in a fallen world, God promised them wonderful blessings if they kept their side of the covenant and lived in obedience to His laws. He said, 'I will take away sickness from among you, and none will miscarry or be barren in your land' (vv. 25–26; it is interesting to notice here that sickness and fertility problems are grouped together as if one problem).

Children *are* a great blessing, and in the Old Testament Wisdom Literature are even described as a 'reward'. Indeed, we considered in Chapter 1 the potentially difficult impact of Psalm 127:3–5 on a childless couple. We can note, however, that during the economic and political situation of those days, the patriarchs of large families were thought to be especially blessed by God. This was particularly so if the man had sons, partly because they would enable abundant production on the land and provide added protection against enemies. Seven was considered to be the number of completeness. God also promised the children of Israel, conditional on their obedience to His laws, to soften or remove other horrendous aspects of life in this fallen world. He would bless them with prosperity in food and drink and drive out their enemies. But it is vital to remember that these physical promises of blessing were given at this *one particular point* in the history of God's people, and *under this historic covenant agreement*. As Christians living under the new covenant today, our application of these promises must be governed by the New Testament and is different (more of that later).

When considering the Psalms (plus Proverbs, Ecclesiastes and the Song of Songs) it is also important to remember that they are Wisdom Literature. In that genre God is describing the *general* way of things as they proceed in life; He is not giving us all 'blanket' promises. Generally speaking, living a God-honouring life results in some physical blessings in this world. But the blessings vary. So the declaration in Psalm 127:3 that children are a 'reward' is not going to mean that every faithful Christian couple will be blessed with a harmonious and healthy family of their own. *Many* will, but never *all*. As an interesting aside, if we read the entire psalm we notice that verse 2b declares, 'He grants sleep to those He loves.' I know many godly Christians who suffer with sleep problems, especially those with young children. Surely nobody would suggest that such people were unloved by God?

Furthermore, we know that Israel as a nation broke their covenant agreement with God almost as soon as it was made and so as a nation forfeited the right to these physical blessings anyway. Any godly Israelite who lived at a later time of plague or famine would have suffered alongside their ungodly counterparts because they were all members of the covenant community.

An interesting incident is described in Numbers 27:1–10. The five godly daughters of Zelophehad were anxious for their father's name to be perpetuated by they themselves inheriting his land, as there was no brother. In issuing a new set of instructions for similar future cases God also made provision for those who had no children at all (vv. 8–9). God knew that the covenant would be broken by Israel, but there is no suggestion in Numbers 27 that those individuals who were childless were under His particular curse. Far from it, as here He was making compassionate provision for their names to be perpetuated!

God remained gracious to His covenant-breaking people and did provide abundantly for them. He gave many children and much economic prosperity to them as a whole. Yet we also see, especially through the Prophets, how in later Old Testament history the nation of Israel as a whole suffered hunger, illness, infertility, tragic deaths of children and conquest by their enemies. Since the covenant was made with the nation as a whole, this was their *collective* penalty for disobedience and covenant-breaking, as had been specifically warned by God in Deuteronomy. We then see how this judgement of Israel as a whole also affected individuals, godly or otherwise. Some godly Israelites, like Samson's parents, were described as 'sterile'. They were suffering from the *nation's* penalty, because they were part of a nation suffering covenant curses. Yet most of the wicked kings described in the books of Kings and Chronicles were obviously not infertile as they produced sons (who often perpetuated or even added to their wickedness). God, in His purposes, had shown those particular kings His undeserved 'common grace' (God's general goodness to all mankind, no matter whether they acknowledge Him or not).

When Jesus came to restore the lost sheep of Israel, He showed them His deity. He ministered among them, partly by restoring some of the original physical covenant blessings. He healed their diseases and gave them food. He assured his followers that the man who was born blind was *not* suffering because of his own or his parents' sin (John 9:1–3) and that the tower of Siloam did *not* fall on certain people because they were more evil than anyone else (Luke 13:4–5). But these blessings brought by Jesus' earthly ministry were only partial and temporary even then. For example, He did not drive out Israel's physical enemies, the Romans, because He emphasized, 'My kingdom is not of this world' (John 18:36). (Interestingly, neither do we have a single recorded incidence in the Gospels of Jesus healing an infertile couple.)

Through His perfect life of obedience Jesus kept and fulfilled the old covenant. By His death and resurrection He ushered in the new covenant. The missionary apostle Paul brought this new covenant to the Gentiles, and so people of all nations can share in it today. As a fulfilment of the old covenant, the new is different. It is primarily a spiritual covenant, in which God's laws are written on our hearts. As Christians we have the Holy Spirit dwelling within us, conforming us to the likeness of Christ. As we saw, Christ did not promise His followers a pain-free life; far from it. He was the Man of Sorrows, and we, walking in His footsteps, share in His sufferings. The New Testament does not say that we today suffer infertility or miscarriage as a specific result of covenant-breaking. Neither does it promise that a life of faithful, loving obedience to the Lord will mean that we are blessed with children—or indeed any other physical blessing. Our reward is in the life to come.

The apostle Paul himself prayed and struggled with a thorn in his flesh, whatever that may have been; but God in His wisdom did not remove it. The covenant promises stated in Exodus (of complete joy, peace, health and fulfilment) will be realized fully only in the world to come. Even Abraham, the first one to have been promised the physical land of Israel and many descendants, was looking forward to his better, heavenly home (Heb. 11:9–10).

So how do we understand what happened to Michal, daughter of Saul? She 'had no children to the day of her death' (2 Sam. 6:23). This statement is made after we read how she upbraided and despised her husband, King David, as he danced in joy before the Lord. It certainly seems that infertility was given as a specific punishment to her. Yet we must remember that again this is *one particular incident at one crucial point* in Old Testament history, the final journey of the ark into Jerusalem. When we look below the surface, as Bible commentators have noted, we realize that David and Michal are representatives of the new and old orders of kingship. King David is representing the new order of holiness and joy. He is God's anointed, a type of Christ, while Michal, 'daughter of Saul' (emphasized much in this passage), represents the old order of ungodly kingship, as had been lived out in the life of her own father and was passing away. Neither she nor Saul appeared to embrace the new order of gladness and utter devotion to the Lord. For this, Saul and his descendants were cut off from the royal line for ever. It is crucial, therefore, that we note this: *nowhere* does the Bible say anything like this: 'So all you childless women, you must have sinned somehow, perhaps even like Michal.' If we are to make any relevant application from this sad tale it would seem more appropriate that we use it as a warning to *all* people everywhere, fertile or not. Surely it is a warning not to despise God's Anointed, but willingly to accept His Kingship in our own lives. As we interpret this story in the light of the New Testament, we can apply it to ourselves in that we must embrace Christ. Otherwise we will be cut off from him and all His blessings in the world to come.

So, then, are all infertile people being punished or judged for some specific sin? Surely not! But many childless Christians have searched their hearts in anguish over this. Most of us know that we are indeed sinners who offend God and others in countless ways. Most of us do know in our hearts that we have no right to any of God's good gifts. Despite all this we aim, however imperfectly, to live consistent lives of godliness and repentance. We do know that sometimes sin has consequences: perhaps even lifelong. As mentioned previously, a few Christian couples may, for example, suffer infertility as a physical consequence of past mistakes. This is a result of our living in a suffering world, and God does not always keep us from the fallout that can result from such experiences. But surely even that is not what we are talking about here. If we, as Christian couples or individuals, have wholeheartedly repented of our sin and known the Lord's forgiveness, cleansing and restoration, Scripture does not teach that we will then suffer punishment (God's wrath or judgement) for our sin. Christ Himself has borne that for us on the cross!

As alluded to before, the Bible does clearly portray the beautiful characters and godly lifestyle of Zechariah and Elizabeth, who were 'upright in the sight of God, observing all the Lord's commandments and regulations blamelessly. *But they had no children*' (up to that point), and 'they were both well on in years' (Luke 1:6–7, my italics). We can see that nowhere here does Scripture suggest that this God-honouring couple were being punished for some disgraceful sin, despite what their society must have believed.

Conversely, we may know some Christians who have walked away from the Lord and have openly disobeyed God's commands, yet whom God has still blessed with children: sometimes even during their time of backsliding! Besides this, if children were actually a reward for holy behaviour or perfectly harmonious marriages, who would have any? Certainly not even some of the Old Testament patriarchs in Genesis, who, although godly, also fell into great sin. Abraham, even after God's promise of a child, gave his wife Sarah over to other men to save his own skin. Sarah herself was not always godly (Gen. 15–21), yet God remained gracious to them both, and Isaac was born. The deceitful Jacob and his bickering, manipulative wives and concubines were together blessed with twelve children who founded the nation of Israel, God's own people. In our own day, we surely know of famously unhappy or ill-advised marriages which have nevertheless produced children. Indeed, it is through God's common grace that He blesses so many who do not love Him or take any notice of Him. He gives them children, yes, and riches, and other wonderful experiences in life. God is gracious in myriad ways to those who do not deserve His favour.

During the covenant days of the Old Testament we note that Hannah appeared to be a godly woman, while Peninnah, from her cruel behaviour and attitudes, seemed not to be. But at the beginning of their story Peninnah already had several sons and daughters, and Hannah had none (1 Sam. 1). Beth Spring writes, 'Hannah was an outstanding, faithful wife. Nothing in the Bible story suggests she was being punished with infertility.'[2] Yet in all these Old Testament characters, both godly and sinful, God showed great grace and mercy in unfolding His plans, especially through the patriarchs. It was through some of them and their descendants that Jesus, the Messiah Himself, was eventually born.

So, if infertility is not a harsh judgement of God upon an individual or couple, what is it? How can we view it? Surely we need to believe that in the life of a Christian couple it is actually part of God's individually tailored, loving plan for their personal good and holiness.

Even infertility is for our good

We have considered how, as Christians, we know that God is our Father, we have been adopted into His family and we have been given glorious spiritual blessings through Jesus. So, then, we may also trust that as a good, wise and loving Father, God knows exactly what is best for us. Throughout the Bible we see that He is concerned primarily with our *spiritual* growth and good.

When struggling with infertility we do not often feel that this situation is for our best. We usually think we have a fairly correct idea of what will be good in our lives, and we cannot understand why God does not seem to agree with us. We might be walking in a perpetual valley of shadow over this for many years. Nevertheless, I have recently begun to understand that these desperately painful circumstances are actually proof that God loves us deeply and with a passion. We know this because He wants us to be holy. God knows that it is for our ultimate best in this world and the next that we will be so. *We* may be consumed with the desire to be happy and fulfilled in this current world, but God knows there is a far better one awaiting us; He wants us to get there, and to be fit for it. Nothing else will give us real joy and peace, as we are urged to remember in Romans 5:3–5: '... We also rejoice in our sufferings, because we know that suffering produces perseverance; perseverance, character; and character, hope. And hope does not disappoint us, because God has poured out his love into our hearts by the Holy Spirit, whom he has given us.' I have often reflected that, even in the natural world, it is often only in deep shadowy valleys that lush growth takes place.

We also understand through Scripture that part of God's loving work of holiness in our lives involves discipline: not harsh arbitrary punishments, but the general training of character by our loving heavenly Father, just as a good parent is concerned for their much-loved child. God wants to develop in us a Christlike character: one of faith, love, trust, contentment and submission to His will. We all, as God's children, are under this loving discipline, in whatever form that may take. Consider Hebrews 12:10–11: 'Our fathers disciplined us for a little while as they thought best; but God disciplines us for our good, that we may share in his holiness. No discipline seems pleasant at the time, but painful. Later on, however, it produces a harvest of righteousness and peace for those who have been trained by it.'

It seems to be that the fire of suffering is often God's way of producing our Christian character. Maybe it is sometimes the *only* way. Perhaps we all know of older Christians who have struggled with the bitterest of providences throughout their lives. Some have known nothing but problems surfacing relentlessly, like waves breaking on the shore. Others have lived without the realization of many of their dearest dreams, and perhaps feel that they have missed out on much that this earthly life seems to offer. Yet they have submitted to the Lord's workings in them during these times, and we can see how beautiful their characters are. A number of years ago, when I was walking through a particularly dark time, God dramatically lifted my vision through a passage in a commentary on Malachi 2–3. It describes the work of an ancient silver refiner. I will quote it in full because it is so awesome:

> You will remember the old-fashioned refining process. The metal was brought to a high temperature so that it melted. Then the impurities in the metal, which have a lower density than the metal itself, would float to the top of the molten liquid and could be blown with bellows from the surface. The process was carefully repeated until there was purity. The beauty of the picture is in the fact that when the refiner of silver had done his work thoroughly then towards the end of the process the thin covering of oxide and the pure bright surface of the silver flashed out. At that point, when all the dross had gone, *the refiner could see his own reflection on the surface of the purified silver* [my italics].[3]

God loves us so much that He wants us to reflect Himself (1 Peter 1:16). He wants to see His beauty and purity, His holy character, shown to the world in us. As with silver refining, this process is indeed sobering: it involves much repetition and, for us, often deep pain. But the picture of the refiner shows to us One who knows exactly what He is doing and who takes the greatest of care. Desiring nothing but the best, He watches constantly and works hard, also at considerable cost to Himself. He will not rest until the work is done.

Interestingly, for our marriage service Nick and I chose for the last hymn 'How Firm a Foundation' (words in Appendix 2). We liked the way that it reflects the Christian life experience and, in some verses, the marriage vows. Verse 5 speaks of fiery trials—and our wedding day none of us really knows what these will be—but also of how the flames shall not (permanently) hurt us. God's design is to remove our impurities, 'our gold to refine'. Indeed, the apostle Paul even says that our faith, which is developed through these trials, is in God's sight 'of greater worth than gold' (1 Peter 1:7).

God's perfect plans for our good also include for us to love Him first and put Him above all other desires of our heart. You probably know Psalm 37:4 very well: 'Delight yourself in the LORD and he will give you the desires of your heart.' Many people apply this in the following way: if we delight ourselves in God, He will give us anything we want (including a baby). Delighting in God is therefore a way of getting something from Him. However, the context of this whole psalm is primarily about protection from difficulties and enemies, and finding peace in the Lord. When reading it through fully we see that we are urged to 'delight', but also to 'trust' in God, 'commit' to Him, be 'still' and 'patient' in Him, and 'hope' in Him. It portrays a relationship of increasing devotion to God when all around is frightening and uncertain. The psalmist conveys that if we make God everything, the prime focus of our lives, and live above all to please Him, then our desire for Him will grow. *He* will actually become *the desire* of our heart! Following this, God will also conform our other desires to match His own.

You probably know Romans 8:28, even by heart. Perhaps, as suggested previously, it may have been quoted tritely or insensitively to you as an infertile couple. Nevertheless, we must still believe it to be true, as God's word to us. We may never know in this life the precise reasons for our individual infertility. We do not know why it had to be this peculiarly painful trial that God is using in our Christian character development.

Neither do we always know whether this particular refining will last us two years, ten years, or the remainder of our earthly lives. But we do cling, even if sometimes very tenuously, to the knowledge that God, in His love for us, knows best as He works out His purposes. He sees the big picture; we see only a tiny portion. And He is good. Should we battle with God's providences for us?

Several years into our infertility journey, I remembered something very significant. A few months before we had actually started trying for a baby I had been struck by something in my personal Bible study. The result of this had been my earnest prayer that God would help me to grow in holiness, no matter what it took. Is infertility and miscarriage one answer to that prayer? Perhaps. And if so, I am, through very faltering steps, learning to submit to this, because I know God is trustworthy.

God is our helper and loving Father

God's Word further shows us that He uses our trials to develop greater faith and dependence on Him, who helps us. Several times in our infertility trial I have believed myself to be at the end of my strength in every respect: physically, emotionally and spiritually. Yet even when I have been so utterly depressed and exhausted that I felt unable to face getting up in the morning, God has been there. When I am devastated at the lack of a pregnancy again, crying myself to sleep for a couple of nights while someone else is joyfully expecting, God has been there. When I have feared for the future and can see it only as being very bleak, God is still there. He has comforted and empowered me. Even when I felt suspended over that black chasm, I did not fall into it. Even though I could not sense God then, He was still there behind it all. I began, albeit very slowly, to appreciate His love again. He held me with indestructible cords which I had not seen at the time. He has always brought us through in the end, and He promises He always will do, such as in Isaiah 41:10:

> So do not fear, for I am with you;
>   do not be dismayed, for I am your God.
> I will strengthen you and help you;
>   I will uphold you with my righteous right hand.

For example, I have had times when, after a night of sobbing, a new day finally dawns and I feel the sun on my skin or notice a simple but beautiful aspect of nature. An old friend telephones and we have a good laugh. Perhaps a family member has contacted us or sent a gift reminding us of their love and concern. I enjoy a moving piece of music on the radio. And I thank God that, even in these small practical blessings, He is showing me, step by step, that He is caring for me and that there is still, in His grace, much enjoyment in this life.

At a deeper level, our sense of inadequacy and lack of fulfilment leave us with an intense ache that only God can fill with Himself. It is for our good that we experience this, for when we are beyond our own capacity to help ourselves and we cry out to Him, He reaches down to us and can comfort and satisfy us in a way that nothing else can. This has been the continual experience of Nick and myself. As mentioned before, I have often questioned why God should allow in me such a hunger to bear a child and not fulfil it. It can seem so pointless a desire. Lydia Brownback was of real help to me over this confusion. She writes:

> Because God loves us, He certainly blesses our lives with lots of good things. He gives us many of our heart's desires and provides for us abundantly. But because he loves us, He also withholds some blessings for reasons that are not always plain to us. So if we set our hearts on what we want God to do for us or on what we think He should do for us, dissatisfaction with life and with God is inevitable.
>
> The primary reasons God withholds certain blessings, the lack of which creates big, empty places in our hearts and lives, is so he can fill those empty places with Himself. He cannot fill with the best what is already full with the mediocre.[4]

One friend of ours who suffered several miscarriages before finally giving birth to her children described her utter desolation at their final miscarriage. The many prayers with which she and her husband had petitioned God in their agony were answered in the negative. In fact, the opposite of each request had actually occurred. My friend reveals how, at that time, she honestly felt such hurt and anger towards God, wondering how, as a loving Father, He could allow this. Could she ever trust Him again? I picture a small child whose loving and reliable father has done something seemingly painful in their life, which they cannot grasp, and although it is for their good, for now they cannot see it. They run to the father, shouting in hurt, despair and indignation, even pummelling him with their puny little fists. I can also see something in that image of myself as I struggled in the months following our miscarriage, and also when languishing in the depths of infertility misery. But as my friend continued (with a hint of Peter's words in John 6:68), 'To whom else could I turn?' Indeed, there is nobody else in the world who offers us the hope, comfort or help that God offers in Jesus. God never abandoned my friend or gave up on her. She can testify to that now, years later. God has promised never to discard any of His children, no matter what our feelings towards Him may sometimes be. In our picture, the loving and all-knowing father simply encompasses his hurt child with strong and tender arms until the storm has abated. When wrestling with God's seemingly incomprehensible providences I try to remember that, just as the human father in my picture knows in love just what is best and right for his child, so our heavenly Father knows the same for us. If we can truly turn to the Lord in our aching need and do not consistently harden our hearts against Him, He will help us through this trauma. He has promised to do so.

At one of our most difficult times, a card from a friend arrived with Deuteronomy 33:27 carefully copied out: 'The eternal God is your refuge, and underneath are the everlasting arms.' This verse, in context, was the final blessing of Moses upon the tribe of Asher. But I and many other Christian friends have also found it to be true in our own lives and experiences.

At a Good Friday service just a month after our miscarriage I was struck by the emphasis on how Jesus at the cross really was abandoned by the Father, in order that we never will be. Those of us who know Jesus Christ as our personal Saviour will never now be abandoned. He will *never* turn His face away from us. It is His promise. Another friend recently reminded me that on some days, perhaps for many days at a time, the clouds are so thick we do not see the sun at all. At those times we can imagine that it has gone, and occasionally we wonder if we will ever see it again. But it is always there, still shining above the cloud and doing us good, even when we cannot see it. And so it is with God. Even when we cannot feel Him or sense His presence, He is still there above everything, and in control. And soon we will see and feel the sunshine of His love again.

Jesus suffered, so He sympathizes

In some respects I do believe that as Christians we are privileged to experience suffering, in whatever form it takes, because we are following in our Master's footsteps. As previously mentioned, Jesus was 'a man of sorrows, and familiar with suffering' (Isa. 53:3). Thankfully, we will never know the unparalleled agonies He experienced for us on the cross. But we do share a little of His life of pain. We know, moreover, that in heaven now He is praying, even pleading, for us.

Crucially, Jesus gives us His Holy Spirit to help us grow in grace and resist sin when we are struggling with unending burdens. He urges us to lay them upon Him. He shares our hurts and sympathizes, because He has been there. He has felt every temptation (or trial) known to us. As Hebrews 4:15–16 teaches,

> For we do not have a High Priest who is unable to sympathize with our weaknesses, but we have one who has been tempted in every way, just as we are—yet was without sin. Let us then approach the throne of grace with confidence, so that we may receive mercy and find grace to help us in our time of need.

I admit that sometimes I have been tempted to think that Jesus may not really understand this problem of infertility because it was not part of His own human experience. But then I have been caused to reflect on the fact that Jesus himself never married or had children of His own. As a childless man who evidently loved children, isn't it possible that He too had a human longing for marriage and His own biological children? Yet a contented family situation obviously was not in the perfect plan for His earthly life. Furthermore, you may recall Jesus' radical, counter-cultural prophesy in Luke 23:29 (that I mentioned in Chapter 10) that the 'barren' women would be considered 'blessed' in a future time of unspeakable national disaster. The very fact that Jesus made reference to infertility in this context suggests to me that He, in His deeply sensitive spirit, had some true understanding of just what those childless women of His day faced. It was only the suffering to be faced by parents on a national and unprecedented scale and with such vehement magnitude that could make infertility seem anything like desirable. Perhaps, as Jesus grew up in Nazareth, He had lived among infertile couples, observing their lives, and His compassionate heart hurt and ached for them in their disgrace and isolation. Certainly when we feel abandoned, misunderstood, lonely, disappointed and in anguish, we can remember that Jesus has experienced these sufferings too, and at a depth we will never know.

Above all, Jesus knew his desperate prayers to go 'unanswered' (or answered in the negative), especially in Gethsemane, when he begged and pleaded for the 'cup' of dreaded suffering to be taken away from Him. By contrast, I for one have never actually sweated blood over any of my infertility trials or prayers. Yet is it not staggering to consider the blessings that came out of Jesus' faithful submission to the will of His Father?

God's plan for each of us is different

It cannot escape anybody's notice that, although God works in all His children, refining and helping them, He does so very differently for each one. As described earlier, this can be one of the most difficult aspects of infertility: to see how other people are given children and seem to be leading very happy and fulfilling lives with them, while we are not. How do we cope with such comparisons without becoming very bitter or disillusioned? I have struggled much with this.

Of course, as mentioned before, some of these people may in later years suffer tragic family circumstances that we definitely would not choose either. We do not know what God will allow, perhaps later, into another's life. What we are sure of is that an amount of suffering is usual for God's children, but just as each of us is unique, so are our trials. For myself I have found that the best way to guard against the comparison trap is to try to avoid comparing myself with others at all. And yet, as described before, it often feels as if the contrast in situations is forced upon us in an unavoidable and very painful manner.

Lois Flowers' book is helpful concerning how to handle painful comparisons. She advocates reading the *Narnia* series of books by C. S Lewis, as they are full of rich spiritual truth and are a great distraction from our infertility problems. Lois explains how *The Horse and his Boy* (book 3 in the chronology) helps us see the mind of Christ over this issue. Aslan is a picture of Christ, and at the end of this particular book he is talking with the young orphan boy, Shasta, about the difficulties and dangers that had occurred in his life. Aslan explains to Shasta why these difficulties had occurred for him. But when Shasta begins to ask about his companion, Aravis, and especially why a particularly painful experience happened to her, he is told in no uncertain terms, 'Child … I am telling you your own story, not hers. I tell no one any story but his own.'[5] This clearly reminds us of Jesus' words to Peter at the end of John's Gospel, when Peter had been asking Jesus what would happen to the apostle John: 'If I want him to remain alive until I return, what is that to you? You must follow me' (John 21:22). As Lois urges in her book, we need to hold fast to this teaching: that what God does in other people's lives is known only to Him, in His wisdom. We need to keep our eyes fixed on what God is doing in *our own* lives. This helped me to begin understanding that as God works out His purposes in all people's lives, part of those plans includes all the pregnancies: wanted, unwanted—and absent. This side of eternity we may never know why one woman falls pregnant easily and why another never will.

In the Bible we are told very little about why certain women did actually conceive with comparative ease. Genesis 29:31 asserts, 'When the LORD saw that Leah was not loved, he opened her womb.' Exodus 1:21 describes how the Hebrew midwives refused to kill the Hebrew baby boys under Pharaoh's orders, and 'because the midwives feared God, he [God] gave them families of their own'. But throughout Christian history there must have been many other unloved wives, and also many courageous God-fearing women, who never conceived. All we know is that God remains wiser than we can ever understand, and He is never mistaken. When struggling with painful comparisons, I often just repeat to myself, 'This pregnancy is God's perfect, loving plan for [another woman's] life. My life is different. My childlessness is God's perfect, loving, refining plan for me.' It does help. It is yet another reminder of how God intimately knows us better than we know ourselves and that He decides what is best for each of us; that He has His reasons, even though I cannot see them. I try also to remind myself that for some women pregnancy and raising a family will itself be a very refining experience.

We often trust in the dark. But is that not what faith is all about? When recently struggling with my very mixed feelings over another new pregnancy, my mother reminded me of the beautiful old hymn 'I Need Thee Every Hour' (words in Appendix 2). Rising above the difficulties of comparisons, and dealing with them in a godly manner, is not something we can do alone; we need to pray for constant help from the Holy Spirit. There are times when news of a new pregnancy is so difficult to hear that all I can do is repeatedly plead with God to give me grace for a sanctified response.

Unanswered prayer?

As mentioned previously, unanswered prayer is one of the major spiritual problems for many Christian infertile couples. We may feel that our prayers for a baby are hitting a blank wall. We are disappointed and deeply hurt, as it seems that God has turned away and is deaf to our cries. We might eventually need to accept that having a baby of our own simply may not be God's plan for us as a couple. If that is so, then all our prayers and those of others for that outcome will never be answered in the way we have wanted. One aspect of our miscarriage that I struggled over most was that God did not answer our earnest prayers to preserve the life of our child. Sometimes we are sorely tempted to wonder if praying will make any difference to a situation. Why pray, we may wonder, if God has already decreed the outcome?

Recently I was challenged by a comment in the book *Mountain Rain*, the life story of James Fraser, pioneer missionary to the Lisu tribes of China and Burma. He himself was quoting from the testimony of a Dr Stuart Holden:

> He said that one of the greatest blessings of his life had been his unanswered prayers. And I can say the same … unanswered prayers have taught me to seek the Lord's will instead of my own. I suppose we have most of us had such experiences. We have prayed and prayed, and no answer has come. The heavens above us have been as brass. Yea, blessed brass if it has taught us to sink a little more of this ever-present self of ours into the Cross of Christ.[6]

It is challenging to consider that when our persistent prayers are not answered as we would wish, even if they are 'noble' desires, we must then pray that God would conform our minds and our hearts' desires to match those of Himself. The Bible assures us that God does answer our prayers and, as in the old Sunday school illustration, His answer may be a joyful 'yes' or a cautious 'wait'. However, the answers to some of our particular prayers are obviously sometimes 'no', and this may be so even if hundreds of people have been praying for a different outcome. As a friend assured me recently, 'God does answer our prayers, but just not always in the way we expect.'

God knows that Nick and I deeply desire to be parents. We have pleaded with Him numerous times. So have many others on our behalf. We know He will positively answer those prayers if it is His will. We are sure that, for a while, it was right and good to bring these overwhelming longings to the Lord in this way. He urges us to bring our prayers and requests to Him, and He knows our desires more than anyone else does. But Nick and I rarely pray for a baby now. After all these years we do not want to 'waste' the remainder of our lives by obsessing over prayers for this when it now seems that God wants us to turn our minds to other things. Neither do we actually want to 'force' God's hand (were that ever possible) to give us a child if it is not actually best and right for us. The apostle Paul prayed about his unexplained problem, his 'thorn in the flesh', three times (as described in 2 Cor. 12:7–10). Then he left the issue with God, knowing that His grace was 'sufficient'. We have prayed for a baby much more than three times! Yet in turning the thrust of our prayers away from the 'family' issue now, we long to know the blessing of minds and hearts increasingly in tune with the Lord and really wanting His other purposes to be fulfilled in our lives.

Furthermore, Nick and I are encouraged as we look back over the last ten years as we can see how God has graciously answered our *other* earnest prayers. We can see how God has picked us up (eventually), set us on our feet again and enabled us to continue living, even with a renewed sense of purpose. He has answered prayers for us to be gracious in situations where we have been sorely pushed. He has answered prayers enabling us to rejoice with fertile couples in the births of their children and to say the right thing. He has often given us help at just the right time, which has helped prevent us sliding into total despondency. He has answered prayer by giving us the inexplicable comfort that only He is capable of giving. He had previously answered prayer that the pain might lessen and even that our desire for a family might lessen, if that was never to be in His plan for us. We currently pray this may happen again eventually, if we are never actually to have a baby. God has done in all these things what has seemed to us at times to be the impossible.

If you are suffering with feeling God to be distant in your infertility prayers, try to remember that God does see. In His compassion, He notices everything: from all the pinpricks of hurt and indignation which are too numerous to mention, right through to the gut-wrenching pain that can threaten to sweep you away at times. We would urge you to talk with Him! Unburden yourself to God; He longs for you to come to Him so that He can begin to work His comfort and help. Do not stay away in your own little ball of hurt, no matter how comfortable that may initially seem to be.

It is our prayer that in all our pain and disappointment Nick and I may, in the end, also be enabled to say to God, 'Yet not as I will, but as you will', and to be fully at peace with His plan for us. We hope to be enabled to trust Him for our uncertain future. We hope to remember that in our old age and death, even if that is lonely and physically difficult, *God* will be with us, and will help and comfort us as He has done so far. He will not let us down in the future. Remember how He promised Isaiah:

> Even to your old age and grey hairs
> I am he, I am he who will sustain you.
> I have made you and I will carry you;
> I will sustain you and I will rescue you.
>
> (Isa. 46:4)

The hymn 'He Giveth More Grace When the Burdens Grow Greater' (words in Appendix 2) has become very precious to us over recent years.

Job teaches us many lessons about suffering

During the year following our miscarriage I set to reading the book of Job thoroughly. I had been drawn to it as in my time of total spiritual blackness about the only verse in the Bible which I seemed able to recall was Job 13:15, 'Though he [God] slay me, yet will I hope in him.' Job uttered this cry in the aftermath of horrendous personal tragedy, when his friends were failing to convey any adequate help. God proved Himself faithful to Job.

However, it is also sobering to realize just how much Job did suffer. If I were in the business of comparing myself with another person, I would not wish to be in Job's shoes. In a very short time he lost all his wealth, his seven children and his health (he is described in Job 2 as having become almost physically unrecognizable). His despairing wife tempted him to end it all, and his friends accused him of gross sin, to be suffering so. I have not suffered to that extent, but you may remember that during our miscarriage

I felt that someone, somewhere, was making things as difficult as they could for me at that time. It is illuminating, therefore, to consider how, with the hindsight of Scripture, we realize that Job's trials were entirely instigated and dealt by the devil, who desired that Job fail spiritually and curse God. In all our sufferings we should be aware that we have an enemy who wishes that our faith should fail. Satan wishes to destroy us personally, our relationships, and, above all, our trust in God, so he will devise numerous traps for us. I have often noted how in our own lives certain small 'coincidences' can occur which make a very difficult day even harder. We must not forget that the devil is evil and may be given by God (in His wisdom) a certain amount of leeway at times.

One highly important message from Job's story is one we have already considered but is worth reaffirming here: Job's horrendous trials were *not* punishment for sin, as his friends insisted. Job himself denied such accusations, and God confirmed this in chapter 42, when He declared to those very friends, 'I am angry with you ... because you have not spoken of me what is right, as my servant Job has' (v. 7).

Another great message in the book of Job is that God remains worthy of our trust and worship because of who He is, not just for what He can give us in the blessings we so long for. Job's sufferings were to prove that his faith in God was not just for what he could get out of Him, as Satan had believed (1:9–11). During Job's time of suffering God spoke to him personally. Chapters 38–41 are simply a grand description of who God is, as shown in creation, from the mouth of God Himself. Our response to this, as shown by Job himself, must surely be to worship God. Despite being pushed to extremes of suffering Job did not 'curse God and die', as had been suggested to him in 2:9. Job displayed his love and reverence for God (his 'fear') even when he seemed to have lost everything. What a great example Job is to us!

We also conclude from this book that God is actually in charge of all things from beginning to end, and that His plans can never be thwarted. The devil will never win any kind of lasting victory; he is a totally defeated, and therefore limited, foe. Job himself testified during his sufferings, 'when he has tested me, I shall come forth as gold' (23:10). God, who knew Job, allowed his almost unbearable trials as proof that faith in God is worth it, and that He uses our sufferings for His higher purposes, such as refining our characters.

When Nick and I were given our first, devastating diagnosis, I remember telling a friend at church that childlessness was the one trial that throughout life I had always thought I would never be able to cope with. Now one of my worst nightmares had actually come true. I trust never to forget her response. She replied, 'Maybe God has given you your worst-case scenario because He is asking, "Sarah, even in *this* trial, will you still love me? Will you still trust me and be faithful to me?"' It is still a challenge for me. We see in the book of Job how God *entrusted* Job with the dreadful experiences and had a high view of Job's faith. Perhaps in our own sufferings we can see God entrusting us with them, as He did with Job. Perhaps we can find some comfort in that.

Pause for thought

- Reflect on how the Lord has encouraged as well as challenged you through this experience. Write down anything specific and perso nal at the moment.
- Fill in the gaps in the following sentences to fit your own circumstances:

  » For the hurt and pain of ... for this I/we have Jesus.
  » For the unanswered prayers of … for this I/we have Jesus.
  » For the suffering of … for this I/we have Jesus.

Bible passages for reflection

Blessed is the man
who does not walk in the counsel of the wicked
or stand in the way of sinners
or sit in the seat of mockers.
But his delight is in the law of the LORD,
and on his law he meditates day and night.
He is like a tree planted by streams of water,
which yields its fruit in season
and whose leaf does not wither.
Whatever he does prospers. (Ps. 1:1–2)

Your word is a lamp to my feet
and a light for my path. (Ps. 119:105)

Great peace have they who love your law,
and nothing can make them stumble. (Ps. 119:165)

Prayer

Lord God, I praise you that you are not a silent, aloof God, far away, distant from us in our pain and suffering. You speak to us clearly and powerfully in the Bible, and draw near to us through it. Thank you so much for your perfect, trustworthy Word. I praise you that all the help we need, all the advice, all the comfort, all the revelation of yourself, we find in the Holy Scriptures. In them I discover your awe-inspiring attributes that show me your holy, incomparable character. I read of your indescribably vast love, beyond comprehension, for me in Jesus. And I read of countless examples where you have shown your faithfulness to your struggling children. While many people make many helpful comments, it is your *Word that is a light to my path. It is* your *Word that brings me the greatest and the most sure and steadfast comfort, peace and happiness. I confess that sometimes, even when I'm most in need of your Word, I struggle to accept your truth. Please forgive me. Help me to delight increasingly in your Word, to hide it in my heart, and to meditate on it day and night, so that I may have greater resources to cope in times of trouble. May I also be better able to bring your help to others. In the name of Jesus, the very Word of God, Amen.*

Chapter 13

Living in hope for today and tomorrow

The purpose of our lives: to bring God glory

We know that the desire for a child can be overwhelming, and yet it is vital that we keep remembering the real goal of our lives, which is to live for God. When I recognize that my longing to have a baby is once again consuming me and I am forgetting about Jesus and all He has done for me, then I know I need Him to help me readjust my sights again. I have found it so easy to proceed through life and completely forget this vital truth. We can still keep on mistakenly thinking that God exists simply to make us happy and fulfilled in the ways we desire the most. But we have seen in Scripture how God longs most that we glorify Him (consider Isa. 43:7). He desires that all our thoughts, words and deeds be honouring to Him, that we live our lives in devotion to Him in response to His love for us—and in whatever circumstances He has placed us, no matter how sad or undesirable they may seem to be. We have considered how our identity and therefore self-esteem are bound up in being children of God. Our transformed lives glorify Him as we live in this sad and sin-sick world, as we thought about in Chapter 11 on 'Developing Thankful Hearts'.

I have found it helpful to note that, as we read through from the Old to the New Testament, there is a subtle shift in emphasis. The Old Testament does indeed focus much on tangible blessings such as the land, wealth, health, family and the visible temple worship. We considered that earlier. Giving birth to children was very important in Old Testament Israel: it was the manner in which God's covenant people expanded and God was revealed to the other nations through the visible signs of His glory. But now Jesus has come and we are in new-covenant days. Now God's own people, His church, is built through conversion: not through physical birth, but through spiritual new birth.

Even though God does still graciously work in human families, very often saving the children of believers, this clearly does not happen in every case. He does promise to save people from every 'tribe, nation and tongue'. So surely it is our mandate as Christians, fertile or infertile, to ensure that all with whom we come into contact have the opportunity to hear the way of salvation. It is our privilege, as believers, to glorify Jesus by witnessing for Him, seeing people turn to Him, then helping to disciple them. They will be our 'spiritual children'.

Carolyn Custis James has written a very positive book about the need for women to learn good theology and apply it in their lives. I was very struck and greatly encouraged by the following thought (which occurs in a chapter about women helping men). She is reflecting on God's command to Adam and Eve in Genesis 1:28 to 'Be fruitful and increase in number'. This is a biblical passage that often causes pain for the childless, but Carolyn urges us,

> The command to be fruitful, multiply, and fill the earth was never simply about populating the earth with human beings but filling it with *worshipers* of the living God. Every child we encounter, every adult we meet, is an opportunity for us to be fruitful, multiply, and fill the earth. Most of us (women and men) can name several godly women, besides our mothers, who have had a major formative influence on our walk with God. Singles and childless women must assume an active role in nurturing children and young people to know and trust God if we hope to fulfil this divine mandate.[1]

Once again, we are looking at producing *spiritual* children here.

The apostle Paul was sold out for Jesus. He lived only for the Lord. Paul's whole life revolved around seeing people turn to Christ and grow in their faith. Reading through Acts again recently I was struck by the focus of Paul's life: his devotion to Christ and the setting of his eyes on things above. He says, 'I consider everything a loss compared to the surpassing greatness of knowing Christ Jesus my Lord ...' (Phil. 3:8). One friend, single and struggling with loneliness (and childlessness), recently shared with me how the testimony of another woman a little older than her was helpful. That woman's life just seemed to be going nowhere at all. Everything kept hitting the blank wall of being alone and dissatisfied. She could see no way forward for her life. That was until the verse 'For to me, to live is Christ' (Phil. 1:21a) became real in her life and experience. When this became the entire focus of her heart, the 'wall' began to recede.

Another way in which God can use our infertility to bring him glory is in our support of others who are also in this painful position. With the infertility statistics continuing to rise, we, as childless couples, are in the unique position of truly understanding the pain. As previously suggested by my friend Lois, perhaps it will be our privilege to use all we have learned to help others who are struggling with life's various perplexing and painful providences.

The biblical women and their husbands whose infertility stories we know something about are Sarah, Rebekah, Rachel, Ruth, Hannah, Samson's mother, the Shunammite woman and Elizabeth. We see in them all how God showed His sovereignty in answering specific prayers, demonstrating that He is in control of conception, is faithful to His promises, and brings hope out of seemingly impossible situations. However, there must have been many more infertile women in the nation of Israel whose stories we do not know. Perhaps there were hundreds, thousands even, who never did conceive. In all the examples of 'miracle' conceptions recorded in Scripture it is clear that God was glorified in countless ways by the outcome. His purposes for the world, and particularly for the nation of Israel, unfolded through them, as patriarchs and deliverers were born, culminating in the ultimate Redeemer, Jesus. Surely this was the prime reason for those 'children of promise' being born: to glorify God. Whether or not *we* shall have children, we pray that our desire would be deepened for God to be glorified in the way He unfolds His plan for our lives.

We have the promise of an indescribable future

Many times over, when the pain of our miscarriage and continuing fertility issues has seemed especially sharp, I have cried to Nick, 'Why? Why such disappointment and heartache?' His answer has often been, 'For a greater weight of glory.' He means in heaven.

Of course, we trust that the intensity of our current infertility pain will ease somewhat as we travel this earthly life. We trust that the Lord will eventually help us to find this true measure of contentment and peace, that we may know other blessings as we centre our lives on living for Him. Perhaps God's plans for us include having many exciting years ahead to be useful for Him. But my friend who was leading the recent ladies' meeting about infertility (referred to earlier) also asked me to summarize what has *most* helped me through these years. It has become this: the certainty that one day the Lord will take me to be with Him. I love to read 1 Thessalonians 4:15–17 and Revelation 21–22, considering that for us who know Jesus, this is the reality of our future.

In case you had not gathered, I love reading, especially social history and biography. Without ever being able to recall all the names, I have noted over the years that other Christian couples in the past were also childless. Many probably never discovered the reasons why. They too may have been deeply sorrowful and perplexed about their circumstances. Some of them may have had family businesses or estates they had worked carefully to maintain, but they left no one to inherit and continue the family name and diligent work. Others may have lived until their dying days in the harrowing shadow of the workhouse, which was the final indignity of having no other family able to care for them. Yet they worked tirelessly for the Lord, trusting Him in their sorrow and disappointment, remaining faithful, and attempting to live lives of useful, faithful service. They, like Abraham, were looking for the world to come. Now they are in glory and are part of that great cloud of believers who surround us and urge us, infertile couples, to finish the race, knowing that the end is more glorious than we can possibly imagine:

> Therefore, since we are surrounded by such a great cloud of witnesses, let us throw off everything that hinders, and the sin that so easily entangles, and let us run with perseverance the race marked out for us. Let us fix our eyes on Jesus, the author and perfecter of our faith … (Heb. 12:1–2a).

As Christians, we are pilgrims in this life, and this world is not our true home. Our destination, our lifetime goal, is to see Jesus! Such thoughts encourage us to keep going.

So, yes, even if we never conceive and bear our own children, or indeed miss out on having a family altogether in this life, we are realistic and admit that there are many joys, blessings and precious experiences that we will never know. But one day we will be in heaven. The counterpart to the apostle Paul's declaration in Philippians 1 'For to me, to live is Christ' follows thus: 'and to die is gain.' Whether we will each face death, or whether Jesus returns before that, once in heaven perhaps we will not remember the pain of this life. If it is remembered, it will no longer have the power to hurt us. That will have been wiped away for ever. All our needs—physical, emotional and spiritual—will be met in ways we cannot comprehend now. There it will not matter whether or not we had children in this present life; indeed, anything we have lacked will be more than compensated. It will be a new order, perfect in every way, where no person will look at another's life and be dissatisfied with their own.

In 1 Corinthians 2:9 we are promised something so wonderful that 'No eye has seen, nor ear has heard, no mind has conceived' its glories. We will also finally be free from sin, from all jealousy, touchiness and unrighteous anger. No one will ever again be frustrated, disappointed or devastated. The day we finally see Jesus face to face, we will be filled with joy and peace and be satisfied for ever. He himself will wipe away every tear from our eyes. Those who were once desolate will sing for joy. We will then truly realize that He is actually all that we have ever wanted and needed. We will have been given the mind of Christ, and so will understand fully all that He allowed in our lives here on earth, and just why it had to be so. We will then simply worship Him for who He is and for all that He has done.

This, the believer's hope, is not far away. We are living with the reality of it now. It is our reason for living and for striving to please God now in this world where we all have many temptations and compounded sorrows. It is promised in the Bible that our tears, obedience in the face of suffering and sacrifices for the Lord's glory will not be forgotten. They will be worth it. For example, Psalm 56:8 describes God specifically noting the 'tears' of His child who is under attack. God will remember, and all our faithfulness will have a bearing on our life in the world to come. Do we not long to hear for ourselves that 'Well done, good and faithful servant!' (Matt. 25:23)? The apostle Paul assures us that all our sufferings in this life are nothing compared with the glory and joy we will experience in the next. It will be 'an eternal glory that far outweighs them all' (2 Cor. 4:17). He assures us that keeping faithful to the Lord throughout our lives will result in 'a crown of righteousness' (2 Tim. 4:8). Peter describes it as 'an inheritance that can never perish, spoil or fade' (1 Peter 1:4).

There is a most poignant passage in Isaiah 56:4–5:

> For this is what the LORD says:
> 'To the eunuchs who keep my Sabbaths,
> who choose what pleases me
> and hold fast to my covenant—
> to them I will give within my temple and its walls
> a memorial and a name
> better than sons and daughters;
> I will give them an everlasting name
> that will not be cut off.

It is deeply moving to consider that even here in the Old Testament, with its emphasis on the many blessings of family life and the importance of descendants, there was an assurance of something *even better* than bearing physical children. God looked upon the eunuchs with the greatest of compassion. He saw beyond the mere outward appearance. They would never marry, and their physical capacity for fathering children had been destroyed. *But for those who loved the Lord and were committed to holiness*, God would add a special blessing. Their lives would still bear fruit in His kingdom. It seems to speak of the present, but most certainly it speaks of the future. It suggests that God had a special place in His heart for these eunuchs, those who had been given no choice in their condition. Their disgrace had not gone unnoticed. Their faithfulness would receive a priceless reward.

Hebrews 4 also describes for us this promise of our eternal rest. But it also contains a warning: that we do not fall short of this wonderful, eternal future, that we do not harden our hearts against God and what He is doing in our lives. A sermon I heard recently was very helpful to me in considering the following. If we still need convincing that God loves us and is not cruel in His unfathomable dealings with us, it must finally and surely be through contemplating this: God has promised, and is preparing for us, this awesome, everlasting future. He sent His Son Jesus to die an indescribable, agonizing death for us, thus securing that future. Through the cross of Jesus God has demonstrated His undying love for us. So why would God be cruel to us in this life? That simply does not fit, does it?

Despite our severe testing, may we keep holding on, straining towards our final goal!

Pause for thought

- Put aside for a moment the hurt and pain of your present situation.
- Write down your thoughts about what God may see in your life at the moment that was not there, or was not so well developed, before you began this journey of childlessness.
- Praise Him for these things.

Bible passages for reflection

Whom have I in heaven but you?
And earth has nothing I desire besides you.
My flesh and my heart may fail,
but God is the strength of my heart
and my portion for ever. (Ps. 73:25–26)

My soul yearns, even faints,
for the courts of the LORD;
my heart and my flesh cry out
for the living God. (Ps. 84:2)

Jesus said to her, 'I am the resurrection and the life. He who believes in me will live, even though he dies; and whoever lives and believes in me will never die. Do you believe this?' (John 11:25–26)

Prayer

Eternally loving Father, from everlasting to everlasting, you are God. You remain the same, and your years will never end. But you have also set eternity in our hearts. We know that, because our Lord Jesus has risen from the dead, we too shall rise to life everlasting. Believing in Jesus, though we die, we shall yet live. O Father, thank you for this awesome and certain hope that you have set before me. My future is to be for ever with the Lord—Hallelujah!

You see all my pain and sorrow. You know all the grief and suffering in my heart. But I praise you that you will more than compensate with the glories you have in store. I cannot understand that now, but I trust your Word. Just one day in heaven will make every grief in this life fade away into insignificance. My soul yearns, even faints, for the courts of the Lord; my heart and my flesh cry out for you, O living God. What can this world offer? Whom have I in heaven but you? O Father, grant me the Christ-centred, eternity-focused grace to say, 'Earth has nothing I desire besides you.' As I meditate on your Word, fill my heart with Jesus, so that the prospect of 'for ever' spent with Him dominates my vision, captivates my inner being and dwarfs every hardship. Whether my life is filled with hope or sorrow, I know that to be with Christ is better by far! Lord Jesus Christ, come quickly! Amen.

Conclusion

So can we really find a lasting peace if we are struggling with infertility? Lois Flowers included a chapter in her book entitled 'Letting Go of the Dream'. She urges us that doing this is important, and that there will come a time when every infertile person will have to do it.

But is it possible to do that? I closely identified with her fear that to do so might mean that an essential part of 'me' would disappear, a part of what makes me who I am. She also admits, though, that to some degree 'infertility will forever remain a part of who you are'.[1] If we have always longed to be parents, how can we release that desire without losing 'ourselves'? How, practically, will the 'letting go' happen? And will all the suffering really have been worth it?

Some couples may experience a decisive event which abruptly forces them to accept that their dream will now never materialize. Perhaps they are given a definite negative diagnosis quite early on in their attempts to conceive. Others may have followed medical treatment which repeatedly failed, and so have given up. Some may have needed radical surgery to be performed, which has since rendered childbearing impossible. Others may have closed the door to adoption or fostering (or had it closed to them). All will eventually reach the menopause. After the initial shock and grief has subsided, such couples may perceive their need to create a new practical focus for their lives. As healing slowly occurs, hopefully they will rediscover, with God's help, the energy and enthusiasm to begin again, as it were.

There are others, however, whose situation is still somewhat uncertain. Perhaps they have endured unsuccessful treatment and have made the decision to forgo any further intervention. Conception is now very unlikely, but perhaps not completely impossible, and that slightly open door can prevent them fully moving on. But as this situation is emotionally unsustainable for years on end, they too will need some aspect of 'closure'.

One friend shared how it hurts to let the monthly 'opportunity' pass by, how it is still on her mind all the time. How painfully right she is; probably it will always be subconscious, ever present until the menopause. But hopefully there will come a time when we will begin to find letting go of this 'optimum time' a little easier.

Perhaps we may also need to cease consciously thinking about what we would have named our children, and dreaming about what they might have looked like. Perhaps in the course of time any little items we have carefully treasured 'for when we have a baby' may need to be put away with our dream: out of sight and out of mind. Perhaps we need to stop waiting for this exciting event of pregnancy, for 'when our lives will really begin', and turn our thoughts more definitely to the life we actually have been given: the life God has for us now. Perhaps we will need to consciously hand our hopes, dreams, our very lives, into God's hands, trusting Him for the outcome. Hopefully, we will begin to be able to pray for God to open up to us some new and exciting opportunities in our service of Him which will help us to start thinking more positively again.

None of this is ever going to be easy, or necessarily happen quickly. But I do know that it is possible to find peace because I experienced it before. I trust and hope that in the goodness of God this will fully happen again. As one friend wrote to us early on in our pain, 'God is a great Healer.' He is 'the Great Physician' who mends broken souls and lives, and in doing so moulds us into the likeness of Jesus. It is His purpose to do so. Yes, I am not the same person I was twelve years ago. But, by the grace of God, I trust I am becoming the person He wants me to be. We try constantly to remind ourselves that endurance in the face of infertility suffering is and will be worth it. We must cling tenaciously to our knowledge of God's perfect character and promises in the Bible. We trust that one day God will return in full the joy we have previously known in Him.

I was speaking very recently to one couple whose painful quest for children ended a few years ago following a hysterectomy. They assured me that the deepest emotional pains of infertility and all its repercussions (the 'bleeding') eventually stop. Slowly the wound begins to heal over, finally leaving a scar. That too will fade over the years, although never entirely, and it may occasionally twinge. But this emotional scar, as with a physical wound, becomes an accepted part of the person. They have learned to live with it.

To have even a hope of this healing, we must surely strive and pray, enlisting the help and prayers of those who love us. We must keep trying to remember that although heaven often seems remote in time and distance, it is actually as real as the world we see here. Indeed, one of our pastors described this present earth as being 'shot through' with the glorious spiritual world. Somehow heaven surrounds us now, as we live. It will not be long before we are fully there. We live for this promise of finally being with Jesus for ever.

Over forty years ago a German nun penned the following beautiful lines. They resonate with my heart. Perhaps they summarize a little of that which I have attempted to share in this book:

> It is difficult for you to accept God's will. God's will seems hard to you. It seems to be ruining your life. Whenever God shatters a life's dream, He wants to build something new on the foundation of a broken heart. He will give you something greater, something more wonderful, for God is love. He never deprives us of anything which really would have been best for our lives. He only seeks to strike the impurities in our life, so that He can build up, in a much more wonderful way, that which lies shattered to pieces before our eyes. He will fulfil the deepest longings of our hearts. Expect that, and you will be able to accept the will of God. Then you will find complete comfort.[2]

Can we trust God, even when suffering through undesired childlessness? Yes, we surely can! We pray that God will help us to experience the truth of this, resounding in our hearts and lives, as we walk the remainder of our days on earth.

An epilogue: September 2015

It is now over three and a half years since the evening of 20 December 2011, when I laid down my proverbial pen and sent *Confessions of a Childless Mother* to Day One. But it is only now that it is to be published. Why should that be?

I had found the writing to be painful, detailed and slow. But it was immensely cathartic. God used the experience to tease out the raw pain, to clarify and refine my emotions, to direct my thinking towards Him through it all. I was given hope for the future. I had begun to find peace.

But God also did what had seemed to be impossible, even unthinkable. Four weeks after the completion of the manuscript we discovered that, against all the odds, I was in fact pregnant again. Despite my intense anxiety and even disbelief, we soon were in the unimagined position of writing to our still-childless friends to explain that we were now expecting a baby, and that this time it looked as if the pregnancy might continue to completion. We pray it was written with all the sensitivity so desperately needed.

At the very end of August 2012, a couple of weeks earlier than expected, yet twelve and a half years after our infertility journey began, we finally held our beautiful little girl in our arms. I had not fully believed, even until then, that it could be possible. We were humbled, unspeakably grateful, and totally undeserving. Again the question came—but now from the 'opposite' side—'Why us? Why should we receive such a gift?'

Pain still lay ahead. We had not known then that severe postnatal illness sometimes afflicts women who have been through a long and difficult infertility journey. And we have found it more humbling than imagined to navigate the path of parenthood. That is another story.

But we are so very thankful. As I began to reread the *Confessions* in final preparation for publication I was shocked to face once again something of the trauma of those years. Apart from a few recent editorial changes and information updates I have left the main content, from the beginning right up to the final appendix, unchanged. It is a snapshot frozen in time, a window into the world of infertility: of desperation, confusion, and yet glimmers of trust suffered at a time when I thought all hope of bearing a child had gone. Some may ask, in retrospect, 'Was it really that bad?' 'Were you really so consumed by it all?' 'Is that really how it is for some who are childless?' Yes, indeed it is. The whole experience made an indelible impression upon Nick and me. We will never be the same again.

Reading our story once more has made me even more grateful for our precious daughter. It has also made my heart ache more profoundly for those very dear to us whose stories have not (yet) ended in the way they long for. To them Nick and I dedicate this book. May they continue to be upheld until that final day, when seeing their Saviour they will hear a resounding 'Well done, my good and faithful servant'.

We also dedicate this book to our darling Abigail, who truly lives up to her name: 'My Father Rejoices' (her mother does too).

Our final dedication is to our little lost one, without whom this book might never have been written. We had prayed that your fleeting life would bring God glory.

Amen. Come, Lord Jesus.

Appendix 1

Helpful resources

Books about infertility

There have been many publications on infertility over the years—more than I could mention here. However, I have found the following to be very helpful:

- Malcolm and Nick Cameron, *It's OK to Cry: Finding Hope When Struggling with Infertility and Miscarriage* (Fearn: Christian Focus, 2005). This book is painfully real. The reader is led through a detailed and graphic account of the authors' infertility and miscarriage experience. I think this book could be an eye-opener for anyone on the 'outside' who wants to understand such experiences better. It also has helpful chapters on keeping marriage healthy. The authors run a website devoted to supporting those devastated by infertility and miscarriage: www.hopewhenithurts.co.uk.
- Lois Flowers, *Infertility: Finding God's Peace in the Journey* (Eugene, OR: Harvest House, 2003). Compassionate, God-centred and realistic, this book was of great help at the start of our infertility journey. I could readily identify with Lois' experiences, and she is excellent at pointing us back to God. This book is also unique as it contains a specific chapter on how Christian pastors can help infertile couples under their care.
- Katherine L. Hall, *Learning to Cope with Childlessness* (Enquirer's Library; London/Oxford: Mowbray, 1983).
- Eleanor Margesson and Sue McGowan, *Just the Two of Us? Help and Strength in the Struggle to Conceive* (Nottingham: IVP, 2010). This is a very broad and balanced treatment of childlessness, with many helpful personal testimonies. Among a wealth of very useful chapters I thought those on 'Real Men Experience Infertility', 'Treatment', 'Lifestyle' and 'Adoption' especially helpful.
- Beth Spring, *Childless: The Hurt and the Hope* (Oxford: Lion, 1995).

Books about bioethics

The following four books are helpful 'primers' in bioethics. I would encourage every Christian to read at least one of them, as we grapple with these issues in the twenty-first century. However, for couples considering fertility treatment, each book also contains important chapters discussing the beginning and uniqueness of human life, together with the issues surrounding reproductive technologies.

- Dr Nigel M. de S. Cameron and Joni Eareckson Tada, *How to Be a Christian in a Brave New World* (Grand Rapids: Zondervan, 2006).
- Dr John Ling, *Bioethical Issues: Understanding and Responding to the Culture of Death* (Leominster: Day One, 2014).
- ———*The Edge of Life: Dying, Death and Euthanasia* (Epsom: Day One, 2002).
- Prof. John Wyatt, *Matters of Life and Death: Today's Healthcare Dilemmas in the Light of the Christian Faith* (Leicester: IVP, repr. 2004).

Other helpful books

- Dr Marilyn Glenville, *Natural Solutions to Infertility: How to Increase Your Chances of Conceiving and Preventing Miscarriage* (London: Piatkus, 2000). Although we are rather circumspect in how much 'self-help' is indeed helpful, this book is very interesting and balanced. Perhaps it is a good beginner in the quest to reach optimum health for fertility.
- Barbara Hughes, *Disciplines of a Godly Woman* (Wheaton, IL: Crossway, 2001). This contains, among other helpful chapters, a challenging section on 'the Discipline of Nurture'. It models to all women, whether they have children or not, how their God-given instincts to 'mother' can be greatly used for His kingdom.
- Carolyn Custis James, *When Life and Beliefs Collide: How Knowing God Makes a Difference* (Grand Rapids: Zondervan, 2001). In the words of the blurb, 'Knowing God doesn't stop the pain, but it makes a difference in how we cope with our heartache' (whatever our heartache is).

Appendix 1

For general devotional reading I have discovered the following books to be very helpful:

- Gary Benfold, *Why, Lord?* (Epsom: Day One, 1998). This is very helpful guidance and commentary on the book of Job.
- Lydia Brownback, *Contentment* (Wheaton, IL: Crossway, 2008). Although this little book is part of a devotional series written for women, there is much in it for men too. There are thirty-two short chapters, each one unpacking a different Scripture passage dealing with the issue of contentment. It is so helpful and challenging, cutting right to the core and then guiding us in how practically to find our satisfaction in Christ alone. If you buy only one of these devotional books, buy this one!
- Nancy Guthrie, ed., *Be Still, My Soul: Embracing God's Purpose and Provision in Suffering* (Nottingham: IVP, 2010). This excellent book is a collection of short pieces on suffering written by various Christians. Tim Keller, Wilson Benton Jr., Helen Roseveare, A. W Tozer, Martyn Lloyd-Jones, Corrie ten Boom, Sinclair Ferguson, J. I. Packer and John Piper, among others, have all contributed insightful and moving thoughts on God's perspective, purpose and provision in our sufferings.
- Steve Terrill, *The Wonder of It All: The Creation Account According to the Book of Job* (Green Forest, AR: New Leaf Press, 2000). This beautiful coffee-table book illustrates God's answer to Job in chapters 38–42. It is packed with awe-inspiring colour photographs, shot by Steve Terrill.
- Paul David Tripp, *A Shelter in the Time of Storm* (Nottingham: IVP, 2009). This is a book of reflections on Psalm 27 which are thought-provoking, comforting and deeply challenging. The author encourages us to consider where our hearts really lie, what we desire most in life, and how God is truly the only answer we will ever need.

Useful websites

For information on the LIFE FertilityCare Programme (LFP) visit www.lifefertilitycare.co.uk.

For access to LIFE's broad range of caring, counselling and information services, visit www.lifecharity.org.uk.

To find a Christian counsellor in your area, try contacting the Association of Christian Counsellors at www.acc-uk.org.

To read specific papers detailing the ethical issues surrounding various fertility treatments visit:

- Care, www.care.org.uk
- Christian Medical Fellowship, www.cmf.org.uk

For details about the new Christian adoption and fostering charity Home for Good, visit http://www.homeforgood.org.uk

Music

Nick and I have found the following (contemporary) CDs helpful recently:

- *Come Weary Saints* (Sovereign Grace) was given to us by a friend after the miscarriage and was a constant companion for a long time afterwards. It deals with the sufferings and trials of life, and urges us to remember how God is always in control and is always good. The songs are all helpful, but I have found 'Hide Away in the Love of Jesus', 'As long As You Are Glorified', 'You Have Always Been Faithful' and 'I Have a Shelter' especially personal.
- *Valley Of Vision* (Sovereign Grace) was inspired by *The Book of Puritan Prayers*. Although the words and music have been vastly updated, this CD faithfully reflects the Puritan mindset of complete trust in God's goodness and His perfect sovereign dealings with us. 'In the Valley' is the first recording on this CD.

The above CDs contain printed lyrics. You can listen to excerpts from the tracks and purchase them at www.sovereigngracemusic.org.

New Irish Hymns (Kingsway) also contains a range of theologically rich songs and hymns written mostly by Keith and Kristyn Getty and Stuart Townend. They encourage us to meditate on God. I especially love 'My Hope Rests Firm', 'Fullness of Grace' and 'Every Promise'.

Source of Every Hour (Cathy Burton, Integrity Music) is also very encouraging.

Appendix 2

Helpful hymns and verses

We have been greatly blessed in the West with a wealth of old hymns passed down the generations, and many of us have some that are especially meaningful in our lives. Below are the words of several which have been precious to me over the last twelve years.

He Giveth More Grace

He giveth more grace when the burdens grow greater,
He sendeth more strength when the labours increase;
To added affliction He addeth His mercy,
To multiplied trials, His multiplied peace.

His love has no limit, His grace has no measure,
His power has no boundary known unto men;
For out of His infinite riches in Jesus
He giveth, and giveth, and giveth again!

When we have exhausted our store of endurance,
When our strength has failed ere the day is half done,
When we reach the end of our hoarded resources
Our Father's full giving is only begun.

Fear not that thy need shall exceed His provision,
Our God ever yearns His resources to share;
Lean hard on the arm everlasting, availing;
The Father both thee and thy load will upbear.

(Annie Johnson Flint, 1866–1932)

How Firm a Foundation

How firm a foundation, ye saints of the Lord,
Is laid for your faith in His excellent Word!
What more can he say than to you he has said—
You, who unto Jesus for refuge have fled?

In every condition, in sickness, in health,
In poverty's vale, or abounding in wealth;
At home or abroad, on the land, on the sea,
As days may demand, shall thy strength ever be.

Fear not, I am with thee, O be not dismayed!
I, I am thy God, and will still give thee aid:
I'll strengthen thee, help thee, and cause thee to stand,
Upheld by My righteous, omnipotent hand.

When through the deep waters I cause thee to go,
The rivers of woe shall not thee overflow;
For I will be with thee, thy troubles to bless,
And sanctify to thee thy deepest distress.

When through fiery trials thy pathway shall lie,
My grace all-sufficient shall be thy supply;
The flame shall not hurt thee: I only design
Thy dross to consume, and thy gold to refine.

The soul that on Jesus has leaned for repose
I will not, I will not desert to its foes;
That soul, though all hell should endeavour to shake,
I'll never, no never, no never forsake!

('K' in Rippon's Selection 1787)

God Shall Alone the Refuge Be

God shall alone the refuge be,
And comfort of my mind;
Too wise to be mistaken, He
Too good to be unkind.

In all His holy, sovereign will,
He is, I daily find,
Too wise to be mistaken, still
Too good to be unkind.

When sore afflictions on me lie,
He is, though I am blind,
Too wise to be mistaken—yea,
Too good to be unkind.

When I the tempter's rage endure
'Tis God supports my mind—
Too wise to be mistaken—sure
Too good to be unkind.

What though I can't His goings see,
Nor all his footsteps find?
Too wise to be mistaken, He,
Too good to be unkind.

Hereafter He will make me know,
And I shall surely find,
He was too wise to err, and O,
Too good to be unkind.

(Samuel Medley, 1738–1799)

The Sands of Time are Sinking

(verses 1, 4 and 6)

The sands of time are sinking;
The dawn of heaven breaks;
The summer morn I've sighed for,
The fair, sweet morn awakes:
Dark, dark hath been the midnight,
But day-spring is at hand,
And glory, glory dwelleth
In Immanuel's land.

With mercy and with judgement
My web of time He wove,
And aye, the dews of sorrow
Were lustred with His love:
I'll bless the hand that guided,
I'll bless the heart that planned,
When throned where glory dwelleth
In Immanuel's land.

I've wrestled on towards heaven,
'Gainst storm and wind and tide;
Now, like a weary traveller
That leans upon his guide,
Amid the shades of evening,
While sinks life's lingering sand,
I hail the glory dawning
From Immanuel's land.

(Anne Ross Cousin, 1824–1906)

I Need Thee Every Hour

I need Thee every hour, most gracious Lord;
No tender voice like Thine can peace afford.

I need thee, O I need Thee!
Every hour I need Thee;
O bless me now, my Saviour!
I come to Thee.

I need Thee every hour; stay Thou near by;
Temptations lose their power when Thou art nigh.

I need Thee every hour, in joy or pain;
Come quickly and abide, or life is vain.

I need Thee every hour; teach me thy will,
And thy rich promises in me fulfil.

I need thee every hour, most Holy One;
O make me Thine indeed, Thou blessed Son!

(Annie Sherwood Hawkes, 1835–1918)

* * *

A few contemporary hymns and songs which I have found very helpful include
'God of the Ages', Margaret Clarkson, 1982
'Wait', Stephen Curtis Chapman and Margaret Becker, 1988
'Blessed Be Your Name', Matt and Beth Redman, 2002
'There Is a Higher Throne', Keith and Kristyn Getty, 2003
Lyrics for these can be found online.

* * *

A moving and beautiful poem, also available to view online, is 'The Divine Weaver' (author unknown)

Psalm 139:1–16

O LORD, you have searched me
and you know me.
You know when I sit and when I rise;
you perceive my thoughts from afar.
You discern my going out and my lying down;
you are familiar with all my ways.
Before a word is on my tongue
you know it completely, O LORD.
You hem me in—behind and before;
you have laid your hand upon me.
Such knowledge is too wonderful for me,
too lofty for me to attain.
Where can I go from your Spirit?
Where can I flee from your presence?
If I go up to the heavens, you are there;
if I make my bed in the depths, you are there.
If I rise on the wings of the dawn,
if I settle on the far side of the sea,
even there your hand will guide me,
your right hand will hold me fast.
If I say, 'Surely the darkness will hide me
and the light become night around me,'
even the darkness will not be dark to you;
the night will shine like the day,
for darkness is as light to you.
For you created my inmost being;
you knit me together in my mother's womb.
I praise you because I am fearfully and wonderfully made;
your works are wonderful,
I know that full well.
My frame was not hidden from you
when I was made in the secret place.
When I was woven together in the depths of the earth,
your eyes saw my unformed body.
All the days ordained for me
were written in your book
before one of them came to be.

Endnotes

CHAPTER 1

1 Lois Flowers, *Infertility: Finding God's Peace in the Journey* (Eugene, OR: Harvest House, 2003).

CHAPTER 2

1 Katherine L. Hall, *Learning to Cope with Childlessness* (London/Oxford: Mowbray, 1983), p. 2.

2 Quoted in Beth Spring, *Childless: The Hurt and the Hope* (Oxford: Lion, 1995), p. 21.

3 Eleanor Margesson and Sue McGowan, *Just the Two of Us? Help and Strength in the Struggle to Conceive* (Nottingham: IVP, 2010), p. 61.

4 The Leeds Teaching Hospitals NHS Trust Print Unit, June 2010.

5 Hall, *Learning to Cope with Childlessness*, p. 10.

6 Ibid., p. 4.

CHAPTER 4

1 Hall, *Learning to Cope with Childlessness*, p. 6.

CHAPTER 5

1 Sheila Stewart, *Lifting the Latch: A Life on the Land* (Oxford: Oxford Paperbacks, 1987), p. 136.

2 Malcolm and Nick Cameron, *It's OK to Cry: Finding Hope When Struggling with Infertility and Miscarriage* (Fearn: Christian Focus, 2005), p. 27.

3 Ibid., pp. 27–28.

CHAPTER 6

1 Flowers, *Infertility*, p. 107.

PART 3

1 Bob Kauflin, 'In the Valley', *Valley of Vision* CD (Sovereign Grace Praise (BMI), 2006).

CHAPTER 8

1 Susan and Tim Ravenhall, 'Making Babies When Sex Just Isn't Enough', 1 May 2010, *The Briefing*; online at http://matthiasmedia.com/briefing/2010/05/making-babies-when-sex-just-isnt-enough/.

CHAPTER 9

1 Hall, *Learning to Cope with Childlessness*, pp. 27–28.

CHAPTER 11

1 Lois Bryan, 'Godly Discontentment?', private paper, 2010.

CHAPTER 12

1 Lydia Brownback, *Contentment* (Wheaton, IL: Crossway, 2008), p. 75.

2 Spring, *Childless*, p. 28.

3 John Benton, *Losing Touch with the Living God* (Welwyn Commentary; Darlington: Evangelical Press, 1990), p. 86.

4 Brownback, *Contentment*, p. 47.

5 C. S. Lewis, *The Horse and His Boy* (New York: HarperCollins, 1982), pp. 164–165; cited in Flowers, *Infertility*.

6 Eileen Crossman, *Mountain Rain: A New Biography of James O. Fraser* (Milton Keynes: Paternoster Lifestyle and OMF Publishing, 2001), p. 93.

CHAPTER 3

1 Carolyn Custis James, *When Life and Beliefs Collide: How Knowing God Makes a Difference* (Grand Rapids: Zondervan, 2001), p. 189.

CONCLUSION

1 Flowers, *Infertility*, p. 178.

2 Basilea Schlink, *Father of Comfort* (London: Lakeland, 1971), p. 37.

Endnotes